Monks
And
Mystics

Chronicles of
the Medieval Church

HISTORY LIVES
VOLUME TWO

MONKS
AND MYSTICS

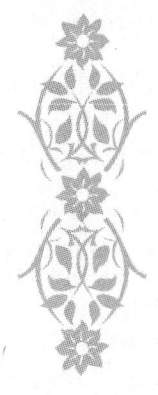

CHRONICLES OF
THE MEDIEVAL CHURCH

MINDY AND
BRANDON WITHROW

CF4•K

This edition © copyright 2005 Mindy and Brandon Withrow
Christian Focus Publications
Reprinted 2007, 2010 and 2011
ISBN: 978-1-84550-083-2

Published by Christian Focus Publications Ltd,
Geanies House, Fearn, Tain, Ross-shire,
IV20 1TW, Scotland, Great Britain.
www.christianfocus.com
email:info@christianfocus.com

Cover design by Jonathan Williams
Cover illustration by Jonathan Williams
Printed and bound by Nørhaven, Denmark

All rights reserved. No part of this publication may be reproduced,
stored in a retrieval system, or transmitted, in any form, by any means,
electronic, mechanical, photocopying, recording or otherwise without the prior
permission of the publisher or a licence permitting restricted copying.
In the U.K. such licences are issued by the Copyright Licensing Agency,
Saffron House, 6-10 Kirby Street, London, EC1 8TS. www.cla.co.uk

For Jonah,
Elizabeth,
Amelia
and Sophia

If you know him,
you too will rejoice.

Contents

Medieval Church Timeline 8

What was the Medieval Church? 11

Gregory the Great: An ape who became a lion 15

How Did the Pope Get His Name? 31

Boniface: The good news of Christ in foreign worlds 35

Charlemagne: Crowned by God 49

What is Islam? 63

Constantine and Methodius: You sent us holy men 65

Vladimir: If you know him, you too will rejoice 81

A Divided Church: The Great Schism of 1054 95

Anselm of Canterbury: May God so reign in your heart 99

What were the Crusades? 119

Bernard of Clairvaux: Did you lead us here to die? 123

Francis: A knight in monk's clothing 141

How the University was Born 157

Thomas Aquinas: We call him the Dumb Ox 161

Catherine of Sienna: Do that which you have promised 177

John Wyclif: I will not die, but live and declare the works of the Lord ... 193

Councils of the Medieval Church 209

John Hus: This goose is not afraid of being cooked 211

Other Medieval Christians 229

The Renaissance: The Middle Ages Come to an End 233

Where We Got Our Information 236

Map 238

Medieval Church Timeline
550-1500

Note: "ca." stands for circa, *a Latin word meaning "around or about."*

553	Second Council of Constantinople
590	Gregory the Great becomes first medieval pope
622	Muhammad, founder of Islam, flees Mecca
680	Third Council of Constantinople
691	Dome of the Rock is completed in Jerusalem
714	Charles Martel becomes leader of the Franks
716	Boniface becomes a missionary
731	The Venerable Bede finishes his *Ecclesiastical History of the English Nation*
787	Second Council of Nicea
796	Vikings invade Ireland
800	Charlemagne crowned Emperor of Holy Roman Empire
851	Crossbow first used in battle
860	Constantine and Methodius evangelize the Khazars
988	Prince Vladimir of Rus converts to Christianity
1000	The abacus is brought to Europe
1054	Great Schism between East and West
1066	William the Conqueror defeats the Saxons at Normandy
1088	University of Bologna founded
1093	Anselm becomes Archbishop of Canterbury
1096	Pope Urban II and Peter the Hermit call First Crusade
1099	Crusaders take Jerusalem
1115	Bernard founds monastery at Clairvaux
1123	First Lateran Council
1128	Order of the Knights Templar recognized by the church
1143	The Qur'an translated into Latin
1144	City of Edessa conquered by Muslims
1145	Bernard preaches Second Crusade, called by Pope Eugene III
1150	Universities of Paris and Oxford founded

1160	Peter Lombard, author of *Sentences*, dies
1179	Hildegard von Bingen dies
1187	Muslim armies led by Saladin retake Jerusalem
1189	Emperor Frederick Barbarossa calls the Third Crusade
1202	Pope Innocent III calls the Fourth Crusade
1206	Francis of Assisi becomes a monk
ca. 1209	Cambridge University founded
1212	50,000 children set out for Holy Land in Children's Crusade
1215	Fourth Lateran Council
1217	Fifth Crusade launched against Muslim Egypt
1228	Sixth Crusade called; Emperor Frederick II takes Jerusalem
1245	Council of Lyons I
1248	Seventh Crusade fought against Egypt
1270	Eighth Crusade called; Crusades end
1272	Thomas Aquinas completes his *Summa Theologica*
ca. 1292	Explorer Marco Polo reaches China
1308	Scottish priest John Duns Scotus dies
1337	Hundred Years War begins
1348	Black Death kills one-third of the population of Europe
1377	Catherine of Sienna convinces Pope Gregory XI to return papacy to Rome
1380	John Wyclif leads a team to translate the Bible into English
1399	Christine de Pisan publishes her *Letters to the God of Love*
ca. 1400	The Renaissance begins
1415	John Hus burned at the stake
1414-1418	Council of Constance
1431	Joan of Arc burned at the stake
1438	Incan Empire in South America begins
1452	Artist Leonardo da Vinci born
1453	Constantinople falls to Muslim invaders
1456	Johannes Gutenberg prints the Gutenberg Bible
1473	Astronomer Nicholas Copernicus born
1475	Artist Michelangelo born
1483	Martin Luther, leader of Protestant Reformation, born

What was the Medieval Church?

THE WORD MEDIEVAL comes from two Latin words meaning "middle" and "age," so the medieval period of history is sometimes called the *Middle Ages*. The words remind us of castles and dragons, knights with enchanted swords, and queens in splendid garments. Historians usually identify the Middle Ages as the centuries between 600 and 1500 A.D. Christians who lived during these centuries are known as the *medieval church*.

Gregory the Great is considered one of the first leaders of the medieval church. But he would not have seen himself that way. Gregory did not wake up one morning in Rome and realize the church had entered a new age. He saw himself as carrying on the work of the early church fathers like Augustine and Benedict of Nursia. But as modern Christians look back on the past, we can see that Gregory's world was changing into a world quite different from that of the church fathers.

THE CHANGING STRUCTURE OF THE CHURCH

If the ancient church is the foundation of Christianity, the medieval church is the house built on that foundation. The early Christians were a scattered band, often hiding in fear of being persecuted for their beliefs. When Emperor Constantine declared Christianity a legal religion of the Roman Empire, the church began to organize into a formal institution. Public leaders were appointed, land was purchased, and beautiful buildings were constructed.

During New Testament times, Jerusalem was the most influential city. But by Gregory's time, Rome had earned that title. At first, the *bishop* of Rome was only one of many bishops overseeing the growing church. But as the church in Rome became more influential over the rest of the world, the bishop of Rome became the most influential church leader. He eventually became known as the *pope* (see "How Did the Pope Get His Name?," page 31).

As their numbers grew, the church needed more leaders. Most cities needed multiple bishops to serve the large congregations of believers. So *archbishops* (like Anselm, Archbishop of Canterbury) were appointed to oversee all the bishops in a given region or *diocese*. The number of regions grew as the gospel spread into foreign lands. The church referred to itself as a *catholic* body, meaning "universal."

Many of the conflicts of the Middle Ages had to do with the struggle between the pope and the emperor (later the king) over who had ultimate authority. Pope Gregory commanded the armies of Rome. Pope Leo III crowned the neighboring King Charlemagne emperor after Charlemagne used his power to secure Leo's position as pope. Bernard of Clairvaux's preaching rallied thousands of soldiers to fight in the *Crusades* (see "What Were the Crusades?"). There was no clear distinction between the church and the state then, like most modern countries have today.

THE DEVELOPMENT OF MEDIEVAL TEACHINGS

While the structure of the church was changing, the teachings of the church were evolving, too. Medieval scholars studied in great detail the writings of the church fathers, and then wrote their own books. The more they discussed these teachings, the more complex these teachings became. Some of their ideas are foreign to modern ears. Some are contrary to the gospel. It is often hard for modern Christians to remember that the people who developed these ideas were studying the Bible in the medieval world—a world very different from today. It would be centuries before the *Protestant Reformation*, a time beginning in the 1500s when many Christians protested some of these teachings and separated themselves from the established church. The medieval Christians did not see themselves as either *Protestant* or *Catholic* like we do today. They were simply members of a universal Christian body that was growing and changing in many ways.

Modern Protestants disagree with quite a few medieval ideas, but that does not mean that the men and women of the Middle Ages were always wrong or that they did not love God's Word. In fact, despite their differences, later Protestants admired many medieval thinkers like Bernard of Clairvaux and Thomas Aquinas. Like Christians of all eras, they made both positive and negative contributions to the church.

MONKS AND MYSTICS

The Middle Ages are dominated by the rise of the *monk* and the *mystic*. Gregory the Great founded Saint Andrew's monastery and became the first medieval pope. Two brothers named Constantine and Methodius left their monastery to become missionaries. Anselm was the *abbot* (a bishop in charge of a monastery) at Bec before he became Archbishop of Canterbury. Bernard of Clairvaux was not only the great preacher of the Crusades, but also the leader of the monastic group known as the Cistercian *order*.

Many of these men and women, like Catherine of Sienna, led a *mystical* life, one focused exclusively on prayer and the spiritual experience. These mystics concentrated on developing an intimate relationship with God.

Some of the people who had the greatest impact on the medieval church were not good role models. Emperor Charlemagne protected the pope and encouraged Christian education, but he also executed his enemies or forced them to be baptized. Prince Vladimir brought Christianity to Russia, but he was a ruthless conqueror who promoted Christ for political reasons instead of a commitment to the gospel. Just as he does now, God used believers and unbelievers from all walks of life to spread the gospel during the Middle Ages.

MEDIEVAL BIOGRAPHIES: FACT OR FICTION

How do we know what life was like during the Middle Ages? Court records and letters that have survived the centuries tell us a lot. But the most common sources of information are *biographies* of church leaders. These "lives of the saints" were the most popular books of the day. Because they were written by people who admired the saints, the facts were often exaggerated to encourage readers to be more like these great men and women of God. This can make it difficult for us to know what really happened and what are just special effects added by the biographers. To uncover the truth, we have to read these biographies carefully, compare them with known facts, and accept the parts that seem most likely.

So be prepared! The world of the medieval church is full of heroes and villains, history and legend. In many ways it is different from our modern world. But the church of today, Catholic and Protestant, traces its roots back to the strange but fascinating Christians of the Middle Ages.

Gregory the Great:
An Ape Who Became a Lion

593. ROME.

GOVERNOR CASTUS SHOVED past the heavy doors of Saint Peter's Basilica. "The Lombards have breached the gates!" he cried.

Hundreds of terrified Roman citizens had crowded into the cluster of church buildings northwest of the city. Huddled along the extensive corridors, they clutched their children tightly, praying that the enemy might show mercy.

Castus found a deacon in the atrium who was trying to distract a group of children with a spinning top. He pulled him aside and said quietly, "King Agilulf is almost to our door. Take me to the pope."

In a tower chamber above the gatehouse, Pope Gregory rose from his knees and moved to the window. It was eerily quiet in the courtyard below. All but one garrison of soldiers had been sent to defend the city gates. The troops who remained had surrounded Saint Peter's as a final layer of protection against the approaching swords. They stood at attention, shields raised, ready to die for their pope.

Gregory willed himself to look away from the row of grim faces. The road in front of the church was deserted. Fearing certain death, the people had fled to Saint Peter's, or to their cellars, stables, or smokehouses—anywhere they might hide from the Lombard army.

An acrid stench hung in the air. Swirling clouds of smoke rose above the city walls, the torched farms and storehouses marking the enemy's approach into the city.

Silently, Gregory backed away from the window and returned to his secluded corner to pray.

"Our Father in heaven, hallowed be your name. Your will be done—." He stopped, took a deep breath, and started again. "Your will be done, on earth as it is in heaven."

A tear ran down his nose and dripped onto his linen robe. "What am I to do, my God?" he cried. "I did not want to be your pope, but you put me here. You have led your people into the wilderness, into a time of sieges and disasters. Now give me the wisdom to lead them out!"

He had been pope for just a short time. Only two years ago, he had been a Benedictine monk serving Pope Pelagius as archdeacon. Then, too, the church had faced an extraordinary crisis. The attacking Lombards were flooding into Rome now, but two years ago, it had been powerful storms and rising floodwaters that threatened to destroy nearly all of Italy.

It had rained heavily for days. Swollen streams in the northern plains rushed down hillsides, emptying into the swollen Tiber River along Rome's border. When the riverbanks gave way, foaming waves surged into the city, etching channels in the streets and carving away ancient buildings. The Romans were forced to their rooftops as the water swallowed their homes.

"As if Rome didn't have enough trouble!" grumbled Pope Pelagius, gripping the arms of his chair for balance as he stood. "Our granaries are washed away and sewage is rising to our windows!"

Surrounding him in his chambers at Saint Peter's were the members of his court, quietly awaiting orders. A young deacon offered his arm to help the pope to his feet.

"Reports from the north indicate that the storms there have carried houses out to sea."

The ailing Pelagius steadied himself with his staff. "If this rain keeps up, Martin, the entire western empire will be under water."

"Rome and the west are no longer the emperor's priority," said a figure, entering the chamber.

Pelagius greeted his friend with relief. "Gregory, give me an update."

Taking Pelagius' other arm, Gregory assisted Martin in helping the pope to the window. "Constantinople is the favorite city now," he whispered.

Pelagius chuckled despite his distress. "Yes, thank you for the politics lesson. I mean an update on our emergency efforts."

Gregory frowned. A man of average height, he had a round face framed with a yellow beard and a receding hairline. As archdeacon, he handled much of the pope's business.

"As long as the war with the Lombards rages on, the emperor won't spare any troops to bail us out," reported Gregory. "The few contingents left in the city were preparing to go north to battle, but I ordered them to stay and help with the relief efforts."

"Good," nodded Pelagius, patting Gregory's shoulder with a feeble hand. "I knew that having a former prefect of Rome in the service of the church would come in handy."

"Yes, but it is my brother, Germanus, who should be given the credit. He's the prefect now."

Pelagius peered at him sharply. "You still object to being archdeacon?"

"I am honored to serve the church of Christ. But I retired from public service for a reason. I would prefer to serve my Lord in solitude at the monastery at Saint Andrew's."

"You are gifted for public service."

"I am a scholar, not a man of action."

It was a frequent discussion. The pope was tired of arguing and clearly had more important issues to deal with at the moment. With an abrupt gesture, he changed the subject.

"The deacons and soldiers shall continue with the rescue of those stranded by the flood," he said. "Gregory, send for your disciples at Saint Andrew's. We'll need their strong hands, and any food supplies they can bring with them."

"We can open up the upper levels of the church," Gregory suggested. "Some of the refugees can stay there until the waters recede."

"If they *ever* recede," Martin said quietly.

Pelagius sighed and stared out the window. "The emperor has abandoned the center of his empire. People are missing. Livestock are dead. A whole season's worth of crops are gone. We've even lost many of our old churches."

"All of Italy may be under water," Gregory insisted, "but God will not abandon the city of Peter."

"You are right, of course," agreed Pelagius, sinking back into his chair. "But the flood is only the beginning."

For weeks the waters flowed through the city. Food was sparse, and many people needed medical attention. Archdeacon Gregory and his aides did all they could to tend to the victims.

Finally, the waters began to recede. Though he was feeble, Pope Pelagius insisted on surveying the damage in person.

Rome was covered in mud. Walls eroded by the water had

tumbled into moldy heaps. Sewage contaminated the streets, attracting rats and flies. The stench of rotting garbage and animal carcasses was putrid.

Pelagius wore a scarf over his nose, but it wasn't a very effective filter. As he shuffled through the city with Martin, the desperate people tugged at his muddy robes and begged for help.

"Please, Papa Pelagius," pleaded an old woman with open sores on her face and neck. "Take my grandchild. I have no food to feed him."

Pelagius nodded to Martin, who lifted the child from her arms.

"I promise you, sister," Pelagius said gently. "We will take care of your grandson."

"Bless you, Papa." She turned away, sobbing.

"I will take him to the closest monastery and see that he is fed and bathed," said Martin. "But how will I find her later?"

Pelagius' pale eyelashes were wet. "You won't, Martin," he said in a low voice. "She won't survive. Leave the child with the monks. They will care for him."

Gregory joined them in front of a house that was in surprisingly good condition. "I've secured several more buildings to turn into makeshift hospitals like this one," he said. "We're moving in the sick already."

Pelagius went to the open doorway and saw people lying on tables, shivering and talking to themselves. "May God have mercy," he said, and moved on.

"Help, Papa! Help!" A man wrapped in a filthy blanket stumbled through the door, shrieking.

The pope went to him. "What can I do for you, my son?"

The man rocked back and forth, mumbling.

"There is nothing you can do for him," Gregory said. "You should continue your survey."

"No!" The man grabbed at Pelagius with a red, sweaty hand. "They're coming!" he shouted. "Stop them!"

"Who is coming?" demanded Gregory.

"*They* are coming! Out of the river and into the city."

"Who do you see?" asked Pelagius gently.

"Angels of death are coming!" the man cried, wild-eyed. "They are coming for all of us!"

A woman caring for the sick pulled the man away. "Papa Pelagius," she called from inside the hospital. "It isn't safe for you to be here."

"This man is suffering from the Black Death, isn't he?"

"Yes. And many others are as well." She pointed. "That man over there is seeing dragons. The woman in the corner is hiding from giant insects. It is not safe for you to be in the streets, Papa."

"She is right," insisted Gregory. "If you stay out here, you will get sick. You should go now."

"Yes," said Pelagius, "but not until I pray for this man." He bent to his knees beside the man and asked God to give him a painless death.

Gregory steered Pelagius back toward Saint Peter's.

"My brother tells me that as a result of the devastation and famine, we can no longer pay our soldiers," Gregory said. "We have no defenses against the continued threat from the Lombards."

"Those unspeakable Lombards!" seethed Pelagius. "The emperor is doing a poor job of defending the empire."

"I've spoken with Castus, but even as governor, his hands are tied. We wanted to open peace negotiations with the Lombard King Autharis, but apparently he just died."

"Then perhaps they will withdraw!"

"No. They continue to advance while a successor is being appointed. But when he is, Castus and I will again pursue peace talks."

"We must pray that you will be successful. As long as our army is weakened and our food is scarce, Rome is not defensible."

Pelagius paused and leaned on his staff. His face was pale and haggard.

"Are you ill?" asked Gregory.

"I will be fine," insisted Pelagius. "I just need to rest. Tramping through the mud takes a bit more energy than this old man has." He looked at the devastation around him and shook his head. "Why would the Lombards want Rome? Not even the vultures wish to be here anymore."

The weeks passed and the ground began to dry out. Houses and stables were rebuilt. But the plague spread rapidly, and thousands of bodies were carried outside of the city to be burned.

The pope's health grew steadily worse and, shortly after the new year, he was confined to his bed. Within days, he was shaking and sweating.

Gregory recognized the grim signs of the Black Death.

Muttering commands through chattering teeth, Pelagius handed over more and more of his responsibilities each day to his archdeacon. One evening, he called for Gregory. Martin found him sitting in his chamber, reading the Rule of Saint Benedict.

"I looked everywhere for you," said Martin, poking his head through the door. "You've been so busy, I guess I didn't expect to find you in the most obvious of places."

"Come in."

"I can't," replied Martin. "Pelagius sent me to find you. He wants to see you right away."

"I know what he wants to discuss," said Gregory, "and I do not wish to discuss it."

"He doesn't have long. You know as well as I do that tonight may be his last!"

"I respect Pelagius, but I do not wish to be God's pope," insisted

Gregory. "I just wish to return to the monastery."

Martin threw up his hands. "That is between you and God and the pope. I have delivered the message, and I have other tasks to do."

Gregory sighed and followed the young man out the door. But before they reached the pope's chamber, they were intercepted by Germanus, the prefect. With a gentle hand on his brother's shoulder, Germanus said, "You are too late. Pelagius is dead."

Within an hour, the bells of Saint Peter's announced the news to the already dejected city. Priests, deacons, and monks filed into the basilica to pray. Gregory was soon surrounded by anxious colleagues waiting to hear his orders.

Hours later, tired and exhausted, he took the first opportunity to slip away from the commotion. But his departure was observed. Germanus quietly followed his brother into Pelagius' dark office.

"Gregory?"

He was met with silence.

"I saw you come in here," Germanus insisted.

"I just want to study Scripture, read, and live by Benedict's rule," Gregory muttered from the corner. "I've had enough of public life."

"This city is in ruins, Gregory! The plague continues to spread. The new king Agilulf of Turin is beginning to gather the Lombard chiefs to take Rome. Our people need their pope!"

"Yes, they do. But I am not the pope."

"Pelagius made it clear that he intended you as his successor."

"I didn't even want to be archdeacon, but Pelagius pressed me into service."

Germanus shrugged. "He needed your gifts, brother. Frankly, we need them even more now."

Gregory closed his eyes, suddenly realizing how tired he was. "I trust in the Almighty God," he said quietly, "but he keeps taking away the solitude I desire most!"

"Forget the solitude, Gregory! God has a lot of work for you." Germanus was insistent, but his voice softened. "He will make you a great pope."

"If it is God's will, then I await a confirmation from Emperor Maurice himself."

Gregory refused to accept the title, but continued to serve the church during the following months. He led the efforts to end the famine and care for those stricken with the plague. But rumors that he would be forced into the vacant position distracted him from his work.

Late one morning, after visiting patients in one of his makeshift hospitals, he returned to the office where he had spent so many hours with Pelagius. The pope's copies of Scripture were still on the desk where he had left them when he had taken ill. Gregory absently ran a hand over the large leather book covers, disturbing a thin layer of dust.

I have heard nothing from the emperor yet, he thought. *Perhaps there is still time to convince him that I am not the right man to be the highest bishop of the church.* He sat down at the pope's desk and opened a pot of ink.

To our most serene lord the emperor, he wrote, careful not to drag his hand across the wet ink. *I understand that you intend to confirm my position as pope, and I ask you to reconsider. My heart is with the simple life of the monastery. I am not ready to handle the problems of the world. You need a powerful leader, not a gentle follower. You are asking an ape to become a lion! I cannot change who I am, even to accomplish this honorable task. Please appoint someone else, and soon.*

He sealed the letter and asked Martin to oversee its delivery.

Martin immediately called for Pelagius' most trusted courier. "Take this letter straight to Emperor Maurice in Constantinople," Martin told him. "These two soldiers will travel with you to ensure that you and the message arrive safely."

Gregory fell into his bed that night exhausted, but with hope. *Once the emperor reads my letter, he will appoint a successor and I can finally return to Saint Andrew's.*

Down the corridor, Martin knelt at his bedside and prayed that, whatever the emperor decided, he would appoint a new pope soon.

And outside, under cover of darkness, the courier and his bodyguards slipped out of the city and headed for the eastern road. But just beyond the gate, they were stopped by a small contingent of the prefect's soldiers.

"You have a letter in your possession," the captain called to the courier. "Prefect Germanus has ordered me to take it."

"The letter is addressed to the emperor, not the prefect," insisted the courier.

The soldiers moved in closer, nudging their horses into a circle. "The prefect insists," said the captain, his hand on his sword.

Glancing from the mounted soldiers to his two bodyguards, the courier finally pulled the sealed message from his belt and threw it on the ground. "The church will not be happy to hear about this!" he cried. He turned back toward the city.

"Hold on," called the captain. "You still have a message to deliver. See that the emperor gets this." He handed the courier a letter, addressed to the emperor, with Gregory's seal. "You will say nothing about this encounter. Is that understood?"

He had no choice. The courier tucked the new letter into his cloak and took to the road with his bodyguards.

The captain turned his horse around and signaled for his men to return to Rome. "The prefect will not let his brother jeopardize the safety of the city by refusing to be pope," he said to no one in particular.

While the counterfeit letter was on its way to the emperor, Gregory called the people to a special service at the basilica of St. John the Lateran.

"He is going to preach a sermon accepting the office of pope," Martin suggested.

But Gregory had something different in mind. He stepped boldly into the pulpit.

"We must repent!" he announced. "Because of our sins and our wickedness, God has refused to deliver us from the plague. We must turn away from our sins and repent publicly. If it is the will of God, he will show mercy."

The people murmured, but they leaned forward to listen, hoping he was right.

"We will pray and sing psalms for three days," he continued. "At the end of the three days, we will gather for city-wide worship. Seven processions will march to St. Maria Maggiore, singing to the Lord and asking for mercy."

For three days, the streets of Rome echoed with prayers and singing. On the fourth day, the people marched from every corner of the city to the church of St. Maria Maggiore, where Gregory urged them to mourn over their sins and pray for forgiveness.

With the support of Governor Castus, Gregory organized volunteers to distribute food and clean water donated by the churches in Sicily. The sick were quarantined, the dead were buried, and the mud was washed from the streets. The clouds of flies began to disappear. The plague was coming to an end.

Meanwhile, the counterfeit letter had reached its destination. Instead of a list of reasons why Gregory was unqualified to be pope, Emperor Maurice read a letter joyfully accepting the position.

Apparently my advisors were mistaken about the situation in Rome, Maurice thought. *No matter. I can't be bothered with a church vacancy while I'm at war with the Lombards!* He wrote a brief reply confirming Gregory as the new pope.

With a groan, Gregory sank into his chair at Saint Peter's, clutching the emperor's letter. "I can't believe this!" he said to the empty room. "The emperor doesn't even mention my objections. It's as though he never read my letter!" *I am trapped. My life will be politics and plagues instead of reading and writing in peace.*

Gregory refused to leave his office that morning. On his knees, he prayed for wisdom. *Perhaps I can flee the city before word of the emperor's letter gets out!* His pulse quickened.

He pulled a simple tunic over his head and slipped quietly out of Saint Peter's. Walking briskly, he tried to stay in the afternoon shadows. He passed a block of houses and turned left at the cross street. Were those footsteps behind him? He hadn't passed anyone. *If I turn around, I risk being recognized,* he told himself, and picked up his pace.

He headed toward the market stalls in the forum. There were few vendors. Many had died of the Black Death, and those who had survived had little left to sell. At least the mud had been swept away. He crossed the square and ducked under a dingy awning.

Footsteps behind him clattered on the cobblestones. Glancing back, he saw half a dozen men crossing the square toward him.

He broke into a run and darted between two vegetable stands. Dodging a bin of half-rotted potatoes, he doubled back and then stopped short.

Blocking his way was his brother. Governor Castus and several men stood a few paces behind him.

"What's the rush?" Germanus gave him a smug smile.

Gregory swung around and saw that he was surrounded. "I'm leaving Rome for a few days."

"We know about the letter."

Gregory threw up his hands. "You also know my objections! I made them clear to Pelagius, I made them clear to you, and I made them clear to the emperor."

"Apparently the emperor never got the message."

"I see." Gregory folded his arms across his chest. "And I suppose my brother the prefect, whose army controls the road, had something to do with that."

Germanus shrugged. "Emperor Maurice requires your service."

"I serve God, not the emperor."

Martin stepped forward from the crowd. "God requires your service to the emperor," he said. "I'm sorry, my friend, but you must accept God's call, for the good of the empire!"

The crowd moved in and seized him then, carrying him back to Saint Peter's. His aides were waiting with fresh garments. They led him into the sanctuary, where the people had already gathered. In a flurry of singing, chanting, and burning incense, Gregory was consecrated pope.

Those were bittersweet memories. *I was fearful and overwhelmed that day*, he thought as he knelt in the tower. *Now I realize that it is God's will for me to be pope, but it seems he continues to test me and the empire!*

"Father, I was short-sighted and disobedient," he prayed. "I didn't want this position, but in your wisdom, you put me here. Now Agilulf is nearly to the door of your house! Deliver Rome from the Lombards. Please show me what you would have me do."

There was a quick knock at the door, and Governor Castus entered. "He is on his way, Great Gregory."

"I know." The pope rose slowly to his feet.

"The prefect and I support any decision you make."

"Thank you. Come with me. I think I can convince Agilulf to leave in peace."

He went out to the top of the wide staircase at the front of the basilica and waited for the enemy to appear.

Outside the gates, the conqueror was shouting orders to one of his generals. "The troops will remain here under your command. Kill anyone who tries to leave the city. And get these animals into some kind of order before I get back!"

He turned his horse around. "Leric, you and your men are with me. There will be no more resistance from these Romans. We take our prize now!"

A shout went up from the grimy, fur-clad soldiers as they raised their weapons high and charged toward the gates.

Agilulf galloped boldly into Rome, his blonde hair streaming behind him. Slowing his horse, he surveyed the spoils of war. The city had not fully recovered from the flooding and plagues of the last two years. The streets were rutted, the buildings moldy, the walls black from his army's torches. Frowning, the Lombard king spurred his stallion toward the looming edifice of Saint Peter's. Leric and his men followed closely on foot. They came to a sudden halt as their commander threw up his hand.

A man in white robes and a tall hat stood atop the massive steps. Around the perimeter, a line of soldiers stood at attention, shields raised in a well-disciplined row. Agilulf's troops snarled at them and shook their bloody weapons, anxious to attack. The Romans waited unflinchingly for the command to charge, but their leader was silent.

Pope and king stared at one another.

"Stay where you are," Agilulf called to Leric over his shoulder. He swung down off his mount and climbed the steps. The Roman troops made no move to stop him.

Pausing a few feet from Gregory, he called out loudly so all could hear. "So you are the cleric who controls the armies of Rome."

Gregory didn't respond.

"I have no desire to kill you," the conqueror stated grandly.

The pope remained still, arms behind his back. "What *do* you desire, Lombard king?"

Agilulf chuckled with surprise. "I think I'm in a position to take whatever I desire, don't you?"

"Do you desire this city?" Gregory demanded with a sweep of his arm. "Rome is not the prize it used to be."

"It is not as beautiful or prosperous as I was led to believe, that is true. But it is still mine."

The pope took a step forward. "Listen to me, young conqueror. To take this city is to take upon yourself a burden that even the Roman Empire does not welcome. Our own emperor doesn't bother to defend us."

Agilulf cocked his head and squinted at his opponent. "What do you propose?"

"I will give you 500 pounds in gold for your spoil. You can boast that you brought Rome to her knees and received a great reward to pay your army."

"I would have taken the gold anyway," Agilulf grinned confidently. "What else do you offer?"

"You won't have the burden of repairing the city."

"How clever."

"And I will personally seek to establish a permanent peace between our people."

Agilulf paused, and looked behind him at his filthy, malnourished men. "I get the gold, the bragging rights, and the opportunity to get my men out of this stinkhole immediately." He flung his bearskin cloak over one shoulder and reached out to grasp the pope's hand. "How can I refuse such an offer?"

Behind Gregory, cries of relief burst from the people crowded in the entrance to Saint Peter's.

The church coffers were opened, and Martin and the other deacons carried out the gold. Gregory's soldiers presented the tribute to Agilulf. Leric's men hooted as they filled their packs with the treasure.

"I will write to the emperor immediately and ask him to begin peace negotiations with your people," Gregory promised.

"I think you are the one who should do the negotiating, Gregory the Great." Agilulf mounted his stallion. "Your people are fortunate to have such a wise ruler."

The Lombard king nodded at the pope, turned his horse, and led his men back toward the gates with their spoils. Governor Castus stepped forward and placed a hand on Gregory's shoulder.

"The emperor will not be happy about those 500 pounds of gold," Gregory murmured.

"That gold purchased the lives of every Roman citizen today. You've done the right thing."

"God has been merciful to this city."

"God has been merciful to the entire empire. I knew you were the right man to be pope."

The refugees behind him began to cheer.

"Send these people home, Castus," Gregory said with a sigh of relief. "And get the soldiers to put out those fires on the walls. It's time we brought this city back to order!"

In 598, the Roman Empire signed a peace treaty with the Lombards. Gregory's role in saving Rome and negotiating peace forever changed the role of the Roman pope.

How Did the Pope Get His Name?

THE WORD POPE comes from the Latin word for "father." Today we use this word to refer to the leader of the Roman Catholic Church, but this was not always the case. The early Christians often called any respected leader of a local church their "father." For example, the Christian martyr Cyprian of Carthage was called "father," even though he did not lead the church of Rome. At first, the leader of the church of Rome was a bishop with the same authority as the bishops in other cities. But since Rome was the head of the Roman Empire, the bishop of Rome eventually became the most influential of the bishops. He often made decisions that affected the rest of the church throughout the world. Soon the other bishops saw the *papacy* as the highest office in the church.

By the time of Pope Gregory I, often called Gregory the Great, Rome had been almost abandoned by the emperor. When the city came under attack from the Lombard armies in the north, Gregory offered the Lombards a peace treaty and saved Rome from total destruction. He united the people in an effort to repair the city, supply food, and help the sick and dying. The pope became nearly as powerful as the emperor.

Like Gregory, other popes had to make alliances with powerful rulers to secure the safety of Rome or their own positions in the church. For example, Charlemagne, king of the Franks, supported Pope Leo III when the pope's enemies tried to overthrow him. On Christmas Day in 800, Pope Leo crowned Charlemagne head of the Holy Roman Empire. Historians recognize this as an important day because it demonstrates that the pope was powerful enough to crown a king. It also demonstrates that kings were keeping an eye on the papacy.

Most of the time, the pope lived in Rome. But during the time of Pope Clement V, the people of Rome rioted over taxes, forcing Clement to flee for his life. He moved to Avignon, France, and that remained the seat of the papacy until the time of Pope Gregory XI. Catherine of Sienna, a sister of the monastic order known as the *Dominicans*, convinced Gregory to return the papacy to Rome.

More than once, people disagreed about who should be pope. This sometimes led to several men claiming the papacy at the same time. Sometimes it created military conflicts.

Many of the popes worked to preserve the church, promote the gospel of Christ, and help the poor. But some were tyrants, who encouraged wars and lived corrupt lives. Some promised what they could not give. For example, during the Crusades, Pope Urban II promised eternal life to anyone who fought for the church.

Why do so many people follow the pope? In Matthew 16:19, Jesus told Peter, "I will give you the keys of the kingdom of heaven; whatever you bind on earth will be bound in heaven, and whatever you loose on earth will be loosed in heaven" (NIV). For centuries, Christians interpreted these passages as Christ's promise to give

Peter special authority over the church. They believed that Peter made a trip to Rome and became bishop there, and that after Peter's death, it was the right of the next bishop of Rome to carry on as head of the church.

Protestant Christians disagree. They say Roman Catholics are wrong to interpret the Bible this way, so the pope does not have the rights he claims. The keys Jesus talked about do not belong to Peter alone, but were given to all of Jesus' disciples (and all Christians after them). The keys are not a power to decide new doctrines, but to exercise authority over believers in matters of church discipline.

We cannot understand the history of the church without understanding the role of the pope. Christian history is incomplete without the stories of the Roman papacy.

Boniface: The Good News of Christ in Foreign Worlds

SUMMER 722. A ROAD IN HESSE NEAR THE RIVER RHINE.

LIKE GIANT FINGERS clutching the moss-covered earth, the roots twisted through the forest floor, converging into a massive trunk that stretched nearly to the clouds. It towered over the hillside, extending a leafy, protective canopy high above the dirt trail.

The three travelers thought it might be the biggest tree they had ever seen.

"There's an inscription," said one, pointing to a stone at the base of the trunk. "What does it say, Bynna?"

Bynna stepped over the gnarled roots and squatted to have a closer look. "It says, 'The Oak of Thor.'"

"The Oak of Thor," the other companion repeated thoughtfully. "We must be close to Geismar now."

"Look," Bynna said. "There are altars back here."

They gathered with curiosity on the other side of the tree.

"It's a sacred grove," said Peter. "The altars are dedicated to Thor, god of thunder and sky, and to the spirits of the trees and the rivers."

"Boniface, come take a look at this," called Bynna, pointing. "Here is an altar to Christ, right in the middle of all these heathen ones."

"Worshiping Christ *and* their pagan gods," said Boniface with a frown. "They're mixing Christianity with the religion of their ancestors."

"I guess I know what you're going to tell them when we get to Geismar."

"That's why we're here." He turned back to the trail. "Let's go. It can't be much further now."

They took to the road again and soon the dense forest began to thin out. Reaching the crest of the hill, they saw before them a village of timber huts surrounded by grain fields and vineyards.

They hailed a boy leading a herd of cows into pasture and asked to be taken to the chieftain.

Chief Otloh was a burly man with a long, braided beard and sun-burned forehead. He immediately invited Boniface into his house and offered him a drink. It was dim and smoky inside the hut, a cooking fire in the center of the one room providing the only light. The young man dragged a bench across the hard clay floor and took a seat near the fire.

"Travelers are welcome in Geismar," Otloh said, handing his visitor a mug. "Where are you and your friends headed?"

"Here," replied Boniface, draining the mug at once. "We intend to settle in this village for awhile."

"And what business do you have in Geismar?"

Boniface presented the chieftain with a packet of letters. "I am here by the authority of Pope Gregory II and Duke Charles, prince of the Franks. These letters grant me safe passage anywhere in the Frankish territories, including here in the Hesse area."

"A friend of Duke Charles is, of course, a friend of Otloh." He glanced at the letters, noting the large, official wax seals. "But surely Charles did not invite you to cross the dangerous Alps just to grow barley with us?"

Boniface laughed. "No. The pope has sent me here to preach the gospel of Christ to your people."

"Ah," said Otloh, raising a bushy eyebrow. He took a second look at his visitor. The young man's hair was cut short in the Roman style, but his features were more like those of the northern peoples. Despite sharp eyes and educated speech, his strong hands showed that he was used to physical labor.

Otloh got himself another drink. "Duke Charles seems to be fond of your pope and his Christ," he said. "But, you see, your journey has been in vain. We have already heard of your god, and many in our village gladly worship him."

"Yes, I saw the altar in your sacred grove of Thor. Who taught you about Christ?"

"A teacher named Scirbald. Like you, he came here to revise our religion. It is because of him that we built the altar to Christ in Thor's grove."

"But the very existence of that grove tells me that you do not understand what it means to worship Christ," Boniface quickly replied. "Christ is not one of many gods to be appeased at pagan altars. He is the one true God."

"Scirbald's Christ is not so jealous!"

"Then I will have to speak to this Scirbald. And explain the truth to your people."

"You have come all this way to get us to betray Thor?" Otloh stood and crossed quickly to the open door. "Since you are here with the duke's permission, I cannot force you to leave. But do not think you can wander into our village and tell us what to believe."

"I'm just trying to save your people."

"Our workers are few. If you want to save us, you can help with the upcoming grain harvest. Good day."

The door shut firmly.

Boniface joined his companions on the road. While he was with Otloh, they had briefly surveyed the village, and now directed him to the only inn.

"There is just enough room for all of us," Bynna said, "and the innkeeper can offer us a hot meal."

"That's the best news I've heard all day," said Boniface.

Over dinner they made plans to split up the following morning and meet some of the villagers. Boniface went to bed early, tired from the journey and eager to begin work.

At morning light, he walked to the village square and watched the town rise from sleep. Singing, a young woman coaxed a cow toward the pastures north of the village. Two men loading a cart with bricks argued over the price of the load. Further down the street, a child began to sweep a doorway with a straw broom, stirring up small clouds of dirt.

Boniface took up a position next to a well at the center of the square and waited. Soon a woman approached with a water jug on one hip and a curly-headed baby on the other. "Good morning," he said.

She nodded. "You're new to Geismar."

"Yes. I'm Boniface."

The child began to fuss, and she juggled him into her other arm.

Boniface reached for her jar. "Here. Let me draw your water."

She smiled gratefully and set down the restless child to play at her feet.

"That carving on your necklace," Boniface said, drawing up the water. "What does it mean?"

"You *are* new here!" She fingered the wooden ornament. "This is the symbol of the spirit of the forest. She brings me good fortune."

"Have you not heard of Christ?"

"Oh, yes. I worship the Christ of Scirbald. And, of course, Thor." She smiled. "You cannot have too many gods looking out for you."

"I'm afraid it doesn't work that way. You cannot truly worship Christ until you destroy your pagan idols."

"Pagan idols? You mean Thor and the tree spirits?" She lifted the child into her arms. "Surely you have seen the great oak in the forest. It is proof that Thor protects this land."

"With respect, madam, it is not Thor who protects you."

"Of course it is! When Thor drops his hammer in the sky, his thunder gives rain to our crops and life to our children!"

"Both the great oak and the rain were created by the true God, not Thor."

She snatched back her jar, and the child squealed with surprise as cool water sloshed onto his bare toes. "Be careful, stranger! Thor does not take kindly to such speech, and neither do his servants."

She marched away.

The rest of the day's encounters ended the same way. He was grateful when Peter and Bynna joined him for dinner at the inn that night.

"We have to pray for wisdom," he said. "This town is as resistant as all the others."

The innkeeper grunted and slapped a loaf of bread and three bowls of pottage on the table.

"I guess the whole town has heard about the 'new' Christian teaching," Peter said.

"Have faith," said Bynna. "Remember Dettic and Deorulf? Their whole village converted within days, and then they even founded a monastery."

Boniface tore a piece of bread from the loaf and dropped it into his bowl. "We certainly can't expect that to happen everywhere we go."

The door of the inn suddenly flew open, and a red-faced man burst in. "Where is Boniface?" he cried. "I demand to speak with him!"

Peter was closest to the door and on his feet immediately. He placed a steady hand on the man's shoulder. "What's the trouble, friend?"

"Take your hand off me!" He shoved Peter away. "Which one of you is Boniface?"

Boniface rose from the table and extended a friendly hand. "I am the one you seek."

"I'm Scirbald," the man replied indignantly. "I have been a Christian missionary to the people of this town for years. What gives you the right to come here and cast suspicion on my teachings?"

"I am a bishop of the church, and I have been commissioned by the pope to deliver the gospel here."

"The pope! We are a long way from the Roman empire."

"Rome is concerned for the souls of all men, not just those of the empire."

"Why should I believe you?"

Boniface pulled a letter from the leather satchel tied at his waist. "Here is a copy of the pope's commission to me. Read it for yourself."

Scirbald glanced at the document, but didn't take it.

"It has the pope's official seal. And see, he mentions me by name." Boniface thrust it at him.

He took the document awkwardly and scanned it without seeing.

"You can't read it?"

The old missionary's eyes flashed. "I do not need to read!"

"How do you teach these people Scripture if you can't read it?"

"I memorized what I was taught."

"That may work for teaching people to sing," Peter interrupted. "But it is no way to convert the town of Geismar."

"I am doing fine without you!"

"No, you're not!" Boniface insisted. "The people in this town have mixed the teachings of the church with their pagan religions. They still sacrifice to false gods and use mediums to speak with the dead."

"Yes, but they also worship Christ!"

"That is not the whole gospel, sir. Scripture doesn't command us just to worship Christ, but to worship *only* Christ."

Scirbald stared at him. "I—I don't know that teaching. I thought it was enough just to build him an altar."

"That is why you must read the Bible for yourself."

Scirbald glanced away, the color rising on his cheeks.

"Don't be embarrassed," Boniface said gently. "I am just a simple man from Wessex. I was taught to read and write Latin, but I did not grow up speaking it. When the pope interviewed me to see if I was qualified to be a missionary, I couldn't speak Latin well enough to answer any of his questions! But he was gracious and let me write down my confession of faith so I could be sure I was using the right words."

"And then he made you a missionary?"

"Yes. He gave me this commission." Boniface took the letter. "*To the devout priest Boniface,*" he read. "*Since you have studied Scripture diligently since childhood and have dedicated yourself to missionary work, I commission you to spread the good news of Christ in foreign worlds. Request what you need for this missionary work and it will be given you. Fare you well. Gregory, servant of the servants of God.*"

Boniface gave the letter back with a smile. "I will teach you to read this."

"Thank you." Scirbald grasped Boniface's outstretched hand. "I accept your offer gratefully."

"The four of us will work together to finish what you started here!"

For weeks, Boniface and Scirbald met every morning to study the Scriptures together. After Peter and Bynna joined them for breakfast, the four of them dispersed to the square, the vineyards, and the fields to preach to the people of Geismar. But there were few converts. Many people said they believed in Christ, but they continued to sacrifice to the spirits of the river and the trees.

"We should ask for a meeting of the village elders," Scirbald suggested. "If we can convert the elders, the people will listen."

They met as the sun was setting, after a long day in the fields. Night insects were beginning their songs in the trees as Chief Otloh built a fire in the square. Fourteen elders gathered around the blaze to hear Boniface's request.

Peter, Bynna, and Scirbald stood behind Boniface as he explained again his commission from the pope and its approval by Duke Charles. When he had finished, Bonnell, the oldest of the elders, rose to question him. The firelight cast flickering shadows on Bonnell's bald head and long gray beard.

"We have welcomed you to our village, and accepted your god," he began. "Why do you insist on preaching to us?"

"I want your people to know the joy of truly worshiping Christ."

"We gladly worship Christ."

"But you still worship Thor and the others."

"Thor is not exclusive like your god, insisting we worship him alone. After all, Thor's children are gods. We gratefully worship them as well."

"Yes, don't you see the problem with that?"

"What problem?"

Boniface frowned. "Think about it. Where does your god Modi come from?"

"He is the son of Thor."

"And where does Thor come from?"

"He's the son of Odin."

"You see? Your gods are not eternal, all-powerful beings. They are born male and female, like humans. They have sons and daughters, and die, like humans. And then you worship their children."

"So?"

"Christ is not such a frail god. He has complete power over his creation. He has always existed. He is the beginning and the end."

"This is Roman doubletalk meant to confuse simple farmers!"

"No," Boniface insisted. "It is the truth. It is the heart of the holy Scriptures."

"We do not value writings the way the Romans do. We value action. We know who protects us, and we will not be so foolish as to abandon him. Thor will reward us for our faithfulness!"

"Hail, Thor!" cried the elders.

"Come on, Boniface," Peter said quietly, taking his friend by the arm. "Things are getting out of hand here. You're not going to convince them tonight anyway."

He grabbed a torch and led Boniface and the others back to the inn.

That night, a storm blew in. Thunder shook Geismar as the rain bent the plump barley stalks back toward the earth. *Thor is angry*, Boniface thought, rising from his bed. He wrapped a blanket around his shoulders. *That is what the people will say. The god of thunder is reminding them who is in charge. Father, how can I destroy the faith these people have in their false gods?*

Destroy. The word reminded him of Frisia, and of Archbishop Willibrord, who had been a missionary there.

He needed to talk. Pulling the blanket tighter, he slipped out of his room and knocked on Peter's door. It opened immediately.

"I can't sleep during storms," Peter said with a shrug. "What are you doing awake? I thought you'd be exhausted after that debate."

Boniface sat on the edge of the bed and stared into a dark corner. "Our mission has been unsuccessful. I have preached, I have argued, I have tried to befriend the people. I'm afraid we might have to try something different."

"What are you thinking?"

"Remember Frisia?"

Peter closed his eyes and sighed. "I was afraid you were going to say that."

"It worked for Willibrord."

"Willibrord took his life into his hands when he destroyed those altars. The Frisians almost killed all of us!"

"But they didn't, Peter. And when the altars were torn down and the gods didn't retaliate, the people realized that they had been wrong for worshiping them."

"I thought you were writing to other bishops and asking for their advice."

"I did. Daniel of West Saxony has strongly encouraged me not to force the people, but to convince them with logic."

"Well?"

"I don't think they will tolerate my logic much longer."

"Give them more time. They have worshiped these gods for generations. It is the foundation of their society. God can change their hearts without endangering all of our lives."

Boniface gazed at his friend's face in the shadows. The rain seemed to be dying down outside. "The storm is passing," he said, standing. "Get some sleep, Peter."

He went back to his room, praying silently. The sun was barely up when the innkeeper threw open the door. "Get out!"

"What?" Boniface fumbled out of bed and reached for his clothes.

"I said, get out! Thor's hammer has fallen. I will not harbor his enemies any longer!"

"The storm was not Thor!"

The innkeeper snatched up Boniface's boots and threw them out the door. "Get out!" he roared.

Bynna nearly ran into Boniface at the door. Peter and Scirbald were waiting for them outside.

"Lightening burned down two trees on the edge of the forest," Scirbald said. "The town is convinced that Thor is punishing them for listening to us."

"They're *not* listening to us!"

"It's superstition, Boniface," said Peter. "They've shared their food and drink with us and Thor doesn't like it."

"What do we do now?" asked Bynna.

"If Scripture and logic and letters from the pope won't convince these people," asserted Boniface, "then we must prove to them that their gods are powerless."

Peter threw up his hands. "Boniface!"

"Our time is up, Peter! We have no choice. Bynna, get an axe. Scirbald, take Peter with you and ask the village elders for one last meeting. Tell them to gather the people and meet me at Thor's Oak at mid-day." He headed to the road, now muddy from the storm.

The sun was high in the clear sky overhead, but little of the light filtered through the dense forest canopy. The shadows were dim around the base of the oak, too dim for the villagers to see the long notch cut low on the back side of the trunk. The air was heavy with the scent of damp moss disturbed by the gathering crowd.

Boniface stood on a giant root, his tunic damp with his morning's labors. Beside him, half-hidden in the twigs and dead leaves on the ground, lay an axe.

Arms folded defiantly across their chests, Bonnell and Otloh faced him at the front of mob. "For what foolishness have you interrupted our work?" Otloh demanded.

"People of Geismar, hear me!" Boniface paused and prayed silently. *Give me courage, Lord.*

Scirbald and Bynna nodded encouragement to him from the back of the crowd. Peter was frowning, but stood protectively close to his friends.

"You have dedicated this tree to a false god," Boniface shouted. "For weeks I have explained the teachings of the holy Scriptures. Yet you refuse to turn away from Thor and the other spirits you worship in this grove."

"You should not say such things in this sacred place," cried Bonnell.

Boniface snatched up the axe and hoisted it over his head. "Thor is a false god!"

The people gasped.

Otloh stepped forward. "It is one thing to tell us about your god," he said in an even tone. "It is quite another to threaten ours."

Boniface looked him square in the eye. "You have left me with no choice."

"The choice you're making now is between life and death. Duke Charles won't hold us responsible if you incite a riot."

Boniface turned away from him and shouted to the crowd. "If Thor is a real god, will he let me destroy his prized oak tree?"

"No!" the people cried, surging forward. "He will strike you down!"

It is now or never, he thought. The villagers were about to defend their god to the death.

"Thor!" he bellowed, swinging his axe at the base of the tree. "I challenge you!"

The crowd froze in astonishment. The clang of Boniface's axe echoed through the trees.

"Stop me if you can, false god!" He struck again. The well-placed blow met the deep notch on the other side of the trunk, and the tree began to wobble.

The villagers watched with gaping mouths as Thor's Oak slowly leaned away from them. It seemed to hover there for a moment, and then the top plunged toward the earth in a green, leafy flurry. Branches shivering, it hit the ground with a thunderous crash, knocking the people off their feet.

When the dust settled, the oak lay in four giant pieces lit by a wide shaft of sunlight. Squinting, the people gazed into a gaping hole in the treetops. Boniface climbed onto the felled trunk and shouted at the sky. "O mighty Thor, where is your power now?"

There was no response from the heavens.

Scirbald jumped to his feet. "Thor is not a god!" he cried.

The forest remained silent. Otloh went to the tree, shaking his head. Something caught his eye, and he reached under a tangled branch and dug out the inscription stone. It was broken in half.

"Thor did not defend himself," he said quietly.

"Thor is not a god," Boniface replied. "There is only one God!"

A smattering of stunned voices repeated him. "Thor is not a god! There is only one God!"

Peter and Bynna ran to the front of the crowd. Finding Boniface's axe next to the stump, Peter swung it at an altar and smashed it with one blow. It was a call to action, and the villagers responded. Overturning the remaining altars, they rushed at the tree with a shout and began to strip the branches.

"Save the wood!" Boniface yelled over their cries. He turned to Otloh with a smile. "We will dedicate the timber to Christ and build a church in this grove."

With tears in his eyes, Otloh dropped to his knees and begged Boniface to tell him more about Christ. That night, Geismar celebrated their freedom from Thor with bonfires and feasts.

Otloh and many others were baptized. And when Boniface set off to take the gospel to the next town, several of the villagers joined his band of missionaries.

Word of Boniface's success spread throughout the Frankish territories, and he made converts in many villages. But it was a dangerous message in a land of many gods. When he returned to Frisia, where he had once ministered with Archbishop Willibrord, the Frisians rejected his challenges to their gods. On June 5, 754, an angry mob massacred Boniface and 53 of his missionary companions. He is now remembered as the "Apostle to the Germans."

Charlemagne: Crowned by God

APRIL 799. ROME.

POPE LEO III DASHED through the streets of Rome. Three boys on a corner stared in disbelief as the leader of the Christian church fled past them, clutching at the pointed miter on his head. An angry mob was close on his heels. "Get him! Don't let him get away!" they yelled.

Only a minute earlier, Leo had been leading a procession of worshipers through the city toward the Flaminian Gate. It was the annual feast day remembering the life of Saint Mark. Praying aloud and chanting the Psalms, the peaceful worshipers were suddenly interrupted by shouts.

"Leo is a fraud!"

"Paschal should be pope!"

Several men brandishing knives emerged from the crowd. The worshipers scattered.

"What pagans are these who disturb the worship of their brothers?" Leo scolded in a commanding tone.

49

"You're a fraud!" the men screamed again, and came at him with their knives.

Astonished, Leo turned and fled.

He dashed toward the gate, but his elegant white robes were not suited for sprinting. They twisted around his ankles and he stumbled. Yanking at the knotted hem, he hoisted the robes over his knees and got back on his feet.

It was too late. The mob tackled him, punching and kicking.

"Cut out his tongue!" yelled a man. "He'll never teach us again!"

"Cut out his eyes!" cried another. "A blind man can't lead others!"

Leo curled into a ball and protected his face with his hands as they slashed at him with their knives. Scarlet stains began to spread across his beautiful robes. Strong hands seized him, lifting him off the ground. With the movement came an intense wave of pain, and he faded out of consciousness.

When he awoke, he was lying on a bed in a dim, quiet room. His head was wrapped with bandages.

"Where am I?" he mumbled. Pain shot through his jaw, and he winced.

A woman's face appeared over him. "He's awake. Get the deacon." She smiled at him. "You're at Saint Peter's, safe for now. Deacon John is on his way."

Almost immediately John was at his side. "It's good to see you awake, Leo. You've been out cold for hours!"

"What happened?"

"Paschal's men tried to kill you."

"That part I remember," said Leo, trying not to move his jaw. "But why?"

"They say Paschal should be pope instead of you. They claim it's his right, since his uncle Adrian was the last one to hold the honorable office."

"I was voted in legitimately by the bishops!" insisted Leo, trying to sit up. He was too weak and fell back on the bed, gasping.

"Take it easy, Father," John said. "Paschal and his brother Campulus have convinced several of the bishops that you have taken the office illegally. The mob tried to cut out your tongue so you would be declared incompetent!"

"Well, at least part of my tongue is still there, because it's so swollen I can hardly swallow!"

"We got to you just in time. Actually, it was this man," said John, standing to greet the young man who entered. "Leo, you remember Abbot Angilbert, the ambassador from King Charles' court? He was in the procession with his guards. They are the ones who pulled Paschal's men off you."

"I am grateful," said Leo.

The young man smiled. "I don't think they'll attack again in public. It won't help their cause for the bishops to catch them harming the pope. But my guards have surrounded your room in case they try to sneak in and finish the job."

"We have to convince the bishops that they have been misled," said Leo. "It will take the persuasion of someone powerful. We must contact the emperor."

"Of course," said John, exchanging glances with Angilbert. "But, Leo, it has been many years since an emperor has shown concern for Rome. And the current emperor is just a boy!"

"His mother might speak on my behalf."

"Empress Irene has her own problems. Under Roman law, she cannot rule legitimately. There is much unrest already. We cannot rely on Constantinople to help you."

"Then there is no one to argue my case!"

Angilbert stepped forward. "No one except King Charles."

"Why would the King of the Franks intervene in a Roman dispute? I know he was friendly with Pope Adrian. And, of course, he sent those lovely gifts with you when I was elected, but certainly his priorities are with his own people far to the north."

"Why do you think I am still in Rome, Leo?" replied Angilbert. "If the king did not have an interest in the affairs of Rome, I would not have been in the procession that day to rescue you."

"Are you saying you're a spy?" Leo demanded, trying again to sit up.

"It's not spying if your intentions are obvious. What does an ambassador do, after all? Charles sent me here to keep an eye on his interests, and those interests include the church of Christ and her earthly leader."

"What difference does it make to him who is pope?"

"You can ask him that yourself," said Angilbert, handing over a letter bearing the elegant Frankish seal. "Pope Leo III, you are summoned to Paderborn to appear before Charles the Great, King of the Franks and the Lombards."

Leo sputtered, struggling to throw off the bedclothes. "No foreign king, no matter how friendly, rules over God's church and her pope. Charles doesn't have the authority to summon me!"

"But he does have the resources to help you," John insisted. "Empress Irene is not going to bother with Rome. Charles is your only ally."

Leo stared at his deacon. "You have already made the arrangements, haven't you?"

"We leave tonight," John replied earnestly. "The governor has offered his personal carriage and driver, so we'll have no interference from Paschal."

"You forget that I can barely move," said Leo, sinking back on the bed.

"I will carry you to the carriage myself. Angilbert and I will both accompany you."

Angilbert rose to leave. "We go first to the Duke of Spoleto's.

He has offered you protection while you recover. When you're well enough to travel, we will cross the Alps and make the longest part of the journey." He nodded respectfully and ducked out the door.

John leaned in close to his friend. "Leo, you must swallow your pride and obey the summons. You need Charles' support."

They left that night as planned and reached Spoleto without incident. Leo regained much of his strength in the duke's hospitality. Within a few weeks, a small caravan headed north, flanked by a contingent of Spoleto's cavalry. Passage through the Alps was difficult enough because of the terrain, but more dangerous were the bands of wandering raiders. John prayed that the journey would be swift and quiet.

"Tell me more of this Charles the Great, called Charlemagne," said Leo, as the carriage jolted along the rough mountain trail. "Is it true that he forces his enemies to accept Christianity?"

"I was a child in Charles' court when he defeated the Saxon rebel Widukind," replied Angilbert. "Charles gave him a choice—baptism or execution."

"And Widukind converted?"

Angilbert shrugged. "He accepted Christian baptism. So Charles spared the lives of all his warriors and made them part of his army." He looked away thoughtfully. "They were conquered by water rather than the sword."

Leo shifted as they hit another rut in the road, adjusting the cushion at his back. "Charles is a compassionate conqueror then?"

"Not always. The Saxons have been raiding our eastern borders for a long time. A few years before Widukind was defeated, Charles lost a number of men in a battle, and in revenge he ordered the slaughter of 4500 Saxon prisoners of war."

Leo put a hand over his eyes and rubbed his temples. "This is the man to whom the church turns for help?"

His companions didn't answer. They finally reached Paderborn.

Abbot Angilbert led them into the marble halls of the palace, where an armed escort was waiting for them.

"You are expected in the king's chapel, sir," the guard said.

John left to see that their baggage was unloaded.

"You will excuse me as well," Angilbert said. "There are many people I wish to see."

At the door of the chapel, Leo was met by a man in a red tunic with gold embroidery at the hems. He knelt when he saw the pope, and Leo noticed that his curly hair was cropped short and covered with a small white cap.

"Roman Father, welcome!"

Leo placed a hand on the man's head. "Stand up, my son."

"The king is expecting you," said the man, rising. "He had urgent business and asked that I show you his chapel while you wait. My name is Alcuin."

"I've heard of you. You are the Saxon deacon who runs Charlemagne's palace school, aren't you? I understand he has a deep commitment to the arts and education."

"I did run the school, yes, but the king recently made me the director of his scriptorium in Aachen. I am responsible for teaching the Bible to young monks, and making sure books, especially the Bible, are copied accurately."

"Excellent," said Leo, nodding. "But why are you not at work in your monastery?"

"I beg your pardon, Father, but news of Paschal's accusations against you arrived many days ago. They say that you rule Rome with tyranny and that you have committed unimaginable sins."

"Lies!" asserted Leo.

"I am the king's theological advisor, so he called me here to meet with you."

"Does he doubt me?"

"Please, Father, walk with me as we talk."

Leo followed him through the chapel, gazing up at the high pointed arches overhead. In the afternoon sun, the colored glass windows along the western wall glowed like giant rubies and sapphires. Alcuin stopped in front of one portraying David and Goliath. In the shadow of the giant, the boy clutched a slingshot and five small stones. Leo wondered briefly if the stones in the window were real diamonds.

"I am sure you know that Charlemagne was raised in a God-fearing home," said Alcuin. "His grandfather, Duke Charles Martel, promoted the work of Boniface the missionary, and sent his sons to school at the monastery of St. Denis. Charlemagne was a nine-year-old prince when Pope Stephen III came to visit the court of his father, King Pepin. Stephen pronounced a blessing on the royal family, and Pepin vowed to protect the church. Now that Charlemagne rules in his father's place, he believes it is his duty to keep his father's vow."

"I am aware that when Charlemagne conquered the Lombards a few years ago, he returned to Pope Adrian much of the land that the Lombards had taken," acknowledged Leo.

"Yes." Alcuin nodded. "Charlemagne supports Rome and will continue to honor the leader of the church. But the charges brought against you are serious. If you are to successfully regain your position in Rome, the accusations must be examined carefully. Otherwise, Paschal will continue to claim that your position is not legitimate. His claims could lead to instability both in Rome and the Frankish territories."

"So Charlemagne's interest in this situation is purely political!"

Alcuin smiled. "The king is a very complicated man. He sees many aspects of an issue."

"And you alone are to examine me and determine my guilt or innocence?"

"Oh, no," said Alcuin, stopping abruptly. "I simply advise the king."

Leo looked intently into the deacon's blue eyes. "And why should I trust you?"

"I am from Saxony, not Rome, so I have no hidden loyalties. And I am protected by Charlemagne, so I have no reason to fear Paschal—or you, for that matter."

"Very well," Leo sighed. "I put my life in your hands."

Alcuin led Leo out of the chapel and, with a nod to the guards at their posts, into the royal court. The beams set in the arches were hung with tapestries. Torches flickered along rows of pillars. Leo's attention was drawn to a massive marble throne in the center of the hall. It was unoccupied.

"This room is normally busy as a beehive," said Alcuin. "But Charlemagne wished to speak with you privately."

Behind them, heavy footsteps echoed on the floor tiles. "Welcome, Holy Leo!" bellowed a deep voice.

Leo turned as a splendid figure dropped to one knee in reverence before him. A luxurious blue cloak fell in graceful folds from broad shoulders. The brown, wavy hair was long and streaked with gray.

Leo placed a hand in blessing on the king's head. "Rise, Great Charles, my son."

"It is an honor to protect you," replied Charlemagne, rising swiftly and towering over Leo. He flung back his cloak, and the pope noticed a fine sword at his side, the hilt glittering with jewels.

"I was just admiring your throne," said Leo.

"I knew you would like it!" boomed the king. "I had it made to the specifications of King Solomon's throne. A little bit of the Bible in my own palace!"

"Your service to the church is unmatched," said Leo. "And yet I must ask you to aid her once again."

Charlemagne gazed at him with piercing eyes under thick brows. "They say you are a tyrant in Rome." The heavy mustache and beard made it impossible to tell if he was smiling or frowning.

"I lead the church as have the popes before me," replied Leo. "When I received the papal office from Adrian, his relatives were furious. They believe it belongs to their nephew and they will do anything to have it. You can still see the scars they gave me attacking me in the streets!"

"What has the Emperor of Constantinople to say about this?"

"While we were at Spoleto, we sent a courier ahead to Constantinople for help. But the emperors have long abandoned the church of the west. Irene and her son are no different."

"They refuse to help?" asked Alcuin.

"The message I received was, *The Pope has his own kingdom to deal with, one higher than mine. Let him take his own revenge*."

The king gestured as if to say that Constantinople was of no significance. "This Paschal has a following, Leo. His charges are serious."

"His charges are false."

"At the advice of Alcuin and others, I have decided to call a hearing."

"Alcuin has explained to me your wishes," said Leo. "I consent, but I cannot return to Rome without being killed."

"Then I will send a small army with you," declared Charlemagne, settling into his throne. "And lawyers to defend you. We will call a synod of your bishops when I arrive."

"You will not come with me?"

"I have other business first. Aachen is threatened by Muslim armies, and minor factions of the Saxons continue to threaten my borders here. Suppressing Widukind didn't end all of the fighting."

"It is true that you forced him to be baptized?"

"You doubt my missionary methods?" The king laughed. "I have no doubt that Widukind was happy to accept Christianity and escape execution, like the other rebel leaders I have defeated. It is a fast way of making converts, my friend."

"You should leave the converting to me."

"And you should leave the fate of my enemies to me. It is my job to defend the church. It is your job to pray for my success."

He clapped his hands, and guards appeared on either side of his throne. "Give the pope and his companions whatever they need to prepare for their return to Rome. Tonight, we shall set aside our troubles and feast together."

"You are gracious," said Leo with a nod. "The church will not forget your labors on her behalf."

Leo and John returned to Rome with an army of Frankish soldiers. But there was no clash when they arrived. Word of Charles' support for Leo spread rapidly through the city.

November arrived in Rome, and with it Charlemagne.

"Where are your accusers?" he asked Leo.

"They refuse to present evidence, but the bishops have been called to a synod anyway. They will gather here in a matter of days. Come, I will show you the cathedral."

Even the Frankish king with his splendid palaces was impressed with the architecture of Saint Peter's. He immediately asked to be taken to the sanctuary. Leo left him kneeling before the altar in prayer.

Rome buzzed with word of Charlemagne's arrival. By nightfall, the city overflowed with attendants, lawyers, theologians, and knights. John and Angilbert stood on the city walls, watching the flickering fires of the army camped outside the gates. Leo prayed long into the night, hoping his tribulations would soon be over. And tucked into his borrowed bed at Saint Peter's, the great king of the Franks snored soundly.

The bishops soon arrived from every region of Italy. On the appointed day, the cathedral was lined with rows of brightly dressed clerics. They flapped like a startled flock of birds as Charlemagne entered, craning their necks to catch a glimpse of the legendary king. Without a glance in their direction, he took his place of honor at the front and nodded to the presiding bishop to begin.

Leo, with John behind him, sat in the chancel next to the bishop. He was dressed in his full papal regalia in snowy white robes and gold-edged miter.

Glancing at the empty seats, the bishop rose hesitantly and cleared his throat. "We are here to review the charges that have been brought against the Holy Father Leo. We are, ah, still waiting for the accusers to arrive."

A whisper ran through the bishops. "Where is Paschal?"

"I am told Paschal and Campulus will be here shortly," the bishop continued. "We will give them a little more time."

Charlemagne leaned over and spoke to an official seated next to him. The man nodded and quietly left the room.

Moments passed. All eyes were focused on the king, who shifted impatiently in his seat and waved another assistant to his side.

"The synod wishes to recognize Charles the Great for his gracious dedication to the church of Rome," said the bishop. "Without his assistance—."

"Enough!" cried Charlemagne, rising from his chair. "The frightened sparrows hide themselves! Where are these men who have wasted our time? Did I bring an army to fight the wind?"

"Mighty king," appealed the bishop, "if we wait just a few more—."

"Nonsense!" Charlemagne turned his penetrating stare on the crowd of bishops. "Is there anyone here who dares challenge the reputation of Pope Leo?"

His deep voice echoed in the chamber.

"Was this man beaten in vain?" the king demanded, striding down the aisle. "Was his tongue slashed and his body stabbed for entertainment?"

The bishops eyed one another, but said nothing.

"Will anyone bring charges against this man, or shall we end this nonsense once and for all?"

The bishops began to murmur. Feet apart, arms folded across his polished breastplate, Charlemagne hovered over the synod.

The presiding bishop resumed his place at the altar. "There is none here worthy to judge the pope," he said.

Leo stood then and walked to the front row of bishops. "If there are no challenges," he stated, "then I wish to swear an oath today that I am innocent."

The presiding bishop glanced at Charlemagne, who had not resumed his seat, and nodded.

Leo raised a copy of the Gospels over his head. "That I may partake of God's promises on the day of the great judgment," he shouted, "I am innocent of the charge that is falsely laid against me!"

"Holy Leo has sworn on the gospel of Christ that he is innocent. What is the finding of this court?" demanded the king.

The bishop looked out over his colleagues. No one moved. He cleared his throat again. "As no evidence has been brought against Leo, this synod finds him innocent," he declared. "Leo is, and shall continue to be, the rightful leader of the church, until the Almighty God delivers him unto the eternal rest."

The king flashed a broad smile at the pope and swept out of the sanctuary. A train of guards and advisors exited in a rush behind him.

Leo found him later, dictating letters to one of his attendants.

"The church thanks you for your assistance," said the pope.

"My father took his promise to your predecessor seriously, and so do I."

"Christmas is only two days away now. Surely you will celebrate the Feast of the Nativity with us in Rome before returning across the Alps?"

"Of course! You are planning the usual services at midnight, dawn, and mid-day?"

"Yes, Rome's traditions will be observed. But with your presence," Leo said with a mysterious smile, "it will be a more glorious celebration than ever before!"

No one, except the powerful King of the Franks, could have guessed what Leo had in mind.

On Christmas Day, Rome was alive with festivities. It was a civil holiday, and merchants deserted their market stalls, laborers set aside their tools, and government officials left their debates. Starting at midnight, thousands of people attended church services with their families and prepared the biggest feasts they could afford.

At the mid-day service, Saint Peter's was packed with Roman citizens, visiting bishops, and members of Charlemagne's entourage. The king himself sat in the front row with Abbot Angilbert at his side as Leo read from the Scriptures.

The pope pronounced a final blessing. Charlemagne rose slowly from his seat and kneeled before the altar, the train of his fur-edged cloak spreading out behind him in a circle of blue velvet. The light of many candles cast a golden glow on his graying curls.

The congregation hushed with curiosity. They did not recognize this part of the Christmas liturgy.

One by one, a dozen of the bishops came forward and spread out across the front of the church at the king's left. A row of Frankish knights in chain mail took their places at his right.

The pope's voice rang out from the chancel. "If the emperor of the east won't rule his people, then you, Great Charles of the Franks, will be the leader of the west."

Leo stepped forward, cradling in his hands a glittering crown, and placed it on Charlemagne's head. "On this Christmas Day, I declare you emperor!" he cried.

The cathedral broke out in excited cries. "Life and victory to Charles!"

The king rose to his full height and turned toward the people, arms outstretched. "I will serve and protect you with all of my might."

"The great peace-bringing emperor has been crowned by God!" Leo exclaimed.

The people cheered and stamped their feet as a smiling Charles marched down the aisle, followed by Leo, the knights, and the bishops.

As they fell into their places in the procession, John leaned over and shouted into Angilbert's ear. "This is the dawn of a new era!"

"You mean the new borders of the empire?"

"I mean the power of the church in political affairs. The pope has just declared an emperor!"

Angilbert grinned and raised an eyebrow. "Ah, but two days ago, the new emperor declared the pope! So which is the true seat of power?"

The cheering crowd surged behind them, and they were pushed out into the street in front of Saint Peter's, where the celebrations had already begun.

Within a few weeks, Charlemagne's knights rounded up Paschal and his co-conspirators. They were tried and found guilty of treason. Charles sentenced them to death, but relented at Leo's request.

In Constantinople in 802, the eastern Empress Irene was overthrown in an uprising led by her treasurer.

With the aid of men like Alcuin, Charlemagne emphasized education and religious reform. His reign became known as the "Carolingian Renaissance." He died on January 2, 814, and left the empire to his son, Louis the Pious.

Leo survived a second revolt after Charlemagne's death and maintained his position as pope until he died in 816.

What is Islam?

THE WORD ISLAM is from the Arabic language and means "submission to God." It is also the name of one of the fastest growing religions of the world, a religion that has rivaled Christianity for centuries. Followers of Islam are called *Muslims*.

The story of Islam begins with Muhammad (570-632), a man who considered himself the prophet of God. He was born in the city of Mecca in modern-day Saudi Arabia. His parents died when he was six, and he was raised by his uncle. When he was 25, Muhammad married a wealthy widow named Khadija and became a successful merchant.

At the age of 40, he began to hear voices and see visions. Wondering what was happening to him, he fled to a cave on Mount Hiram. With the encouragement of his wife and his friends, he became convinced that God's angel Gabriel was giving him an important message.

In Deuteronomy 18:18, God promised to send a great prophet. Jews believed that God had not yet sent his prophet. Christians believed that God had fulfilled his promise when Jesus was born.

But Muhammad thought that they were both wrong, that *he* was the prophet foretold in the Old Testament. He wrote down everything he believed Gabriel was telling him. His writings became the Muslim scriptures known as the *Qur'an*.

Muhammad believed that Jesus was a prophet, but not the Son of God. He said that the Christian doctrine of the Trinity (God the Father, God the Son, and God the Holy Spirit) was a false teaching of multiple gods.

He returned to Mecca and began to preach to the people. He soon made many enemies among the tribal leaders. When someone tried to kill him in 622, he fled to the city of Yathrib (later called Medina). His teachings of peace brought an end to local tribal wars, and he became a powerful leader in Medina. In 630, he returned to Mecca with an army and conquered the city without much of a fight. To this day, Muslims consider Mecca a holy city and travel there from all over the world on a pilgrimage known as the *hajj*.

Muhammad thought his religion would be accepted by Jews and Christians because they are "people of the book," followers of a written revelation from God. Because some of the teachings of Islam were similar to Christian teachings, many early Christians treated Islam as a corrupt version of Christianity. But it became clear that the Qur'an and the Bible do not teach the same doctrines. Christians declared Islam a false religion.

Muhammad's teachings spread quickly across western Asia, North Africa, and Europe. As it spread, military conflicts arose between Christian and Muslim rulers. Both believed that the Holy Land, and especially the city of Jerusalem, belonged to their people. During the following centuries, hundreds of thousands of people would die in the *Crusades* as Christians and Muslims battled for control (see the feature, "What were the Crusades?," page 119).

Today, Christianity, Islam, and Judaism remain the three major religions of the world.

Constantine and Methodius: You Sent Us Holy Men

JUNE 18, 860. THE SHORES OF CONSTANTINOPLE.

PHOTIUS, PATRIARCH OF Constantinople, stood on a wide balcony of the imperial palace and gratefully breathed in the fresh air. Below him, the city stretched out toward the harbor known as the Golden Horn, where several ships bearing the emperor's insignia bobbed on the sparkling surface. The burnished dome of the Church of Hagia Sophia glowed under a blue sky. The world seemed so calm, so quiet. *What a false impression one gets from this distance*, he thought.

Thirty minutes earlier, in response to the emperor's summons, he had torn himself away from the throng of mourners at Hagia Sophia. Plodding through the broad avenues, still muddy from the thunderstorms of the last two days, he passed buildings blackened by fire.

The double set of walls kept the barbarians from swarming into Constantinople, he thought, *but they couldn't stop the wave of fiery arrows launched from enemy ships in the harbor.*

The storm came ashore with the emperor. He and his navy had

returned just in time to rescue the besieged city, but too late to save the outlying villages. Sudden rains quenched the fires, but flooding buried the rubble in mud. Photius knew it would be days before the soldiers recovered all the bodies. Already he and his priests had performed hundreds of funeral rites.

With a heavy heart, he stepped back inside. The emperor's advisors were gathering in the council room.

Basil, one of the caesars who ruled a portion of the empire under the emperor, glared at the patriarch as he entered.

Photius ignored him and took a seat at the table next to General Stephen. "Does Emperor Michael intend to go after our attackers?"

"Fool," hissed Basil.

Photius wasn't sure if the ceasar was referring to him or the emperor. It was common knowledge that Basil had his eyes on the imperial throne. Apparently only the emperor mistook his ambition for loyalty. He pretended not to hear the remark.

"Many of our people are still missing, general," Photius continued. "Perhaps they have been taken prisoner?"

General Stephen rubbed the back of his neck and turned bloodshot eyes on his companion. "The Rus do not take prisoners, patriarch. They simply slaughter and burn everything in their path."

Photius was quiet as the other men took their seats. A private door at the end of the room banged open, and Emperor Michael barged in unannounced. Three attendants followed close on his heels.

"I want to know how this happened!" he demanded, slamming a heavy goblet on the table. An attendant immediately filled the glass. No one spoke.

"Have I hired children to run this empire?" Michael leaned heavily on the table and glared at his council.

"Sir," replied the general, "they came like a wave of the sea. There was no time to——."

"Enough!" interrupted Michael. "I will not accept excuses, only answers or resignations. How did the armies of Rus manage to get 200 ships into the Golden Horn?"

The general dared not suggest it had anything to do with the absence of the navy.

"Great Michael, may I make a suggestion?" asked Basil.

"One of you must have something to say!" Michael threw himself into the chair at the head of the table and drained his glass.

"I believe it is time for us to renew our alliances with the Khazars in the north."

Michael gestured impatiently for the caesar to continue.

"From what our informants are able to tell, our enemies sailed down the Dnieper River into the Black Sea. Along the way, they ransacked several Khazar villages. Clearly they are as much a threat to the Dnieper region as they are to us."

Michael turned to the general with one eyebrow raised.

"The Khazars do stand between us and Rus lands," General Stephen acknowledged.

"So if we form an alliance with the Khazars, we would establish a line of defense between us and the Rus," Basil continued. "In the past we had success when we offered to help them build forts in the north."

Photius shifted uncomfortably at the idea of using their neighbors as a shield. *Still,* he thought, *we* would *be protecting our people* and *helping the Khazars defend themselves. And there are even more important consequences.* He leaned in and addressed the emperor. "The church could be invaluable in building such an alliance."

Michael looked at him in surprise, as the patriarch rarely engaged in military discussions. "Go on, Holy Photius."

"The Khazars are a people of various races. In the Dnieper region, they are mostly Slavic."

"Yes?"

"Our union with these neighbors would be stronger if we

shared a religion. We should send missionaries to the Slavs."

Photius was startled to hear Basil agree.

"The Khazars have moved into the Crimean Peninsula, north of the Black Sea," said Basil. "We still control some of that territory and occasionally trade with local merchants. The patriarch's missionaries might begin there."

"Proceed," ordered Michael.

The general spoke up. "Sir, we should first contact the leader of the Khazars and request permission to evangelize his people. Sending a boat full of missionaries into their community could be mistaken as a threat."

"True," Michael said. "Photius, who do you recommend as an ambassador?"

"There are only two people who could lead such a mission, the brothers Constantine and Methodius."

"The sons of Leo, former governor of Thessalonica?"

"Yes, sir. You know the family?"

"Constantine is a philosopher and a linguist, isn't he? His older brother Methodius governed for a time in Slavic territory before he joined a monastery."

Photius nodded. "The Slavs have been trading in the Thessalonian marketplace for years, so the brothers know their language and customs. Constantine was one of my brightest students when I taught in the imperial school. He knows Christian doctrine. And his brother would be a valuable assistant."

Michael raised a hand to stop him. "Your judgment in religious matters is superior to mine. Where are our new ambassadors now?"

"The last I heard, they were in Bithynia, in Asia Minor."

"Send messengers to search all the monasteries in Bithynia," ordered Michael, rising to his feet. "I want Constantine and Methodius here immediately!"

His attendants followed him out.

It took some time to locate the brothers, and it was autumn by the time they arrived in Constantinople. Photius met them at the palace, where they waited for an audience with the emperor.

"How good it is to see you again, my son!" said the patriarch, embracing Constantine.

His former student was thinner than he remembered, no doubt due to fasting and long hours of copying detailed manuscripts at the monastery. A crease in his forehead and shadows under the large black eyes gave him a serious appearance. But he was smiling.

"I have missed your conversation, Holy Photius," Constantine declared. "Have you ever met my brother Methodius?" He turned to the man at his side.

"We are honored to serve the church and the empire, patriarch." Methodius bent forward in a gesture of respect. He was taller than his brother, and his beard had more gray. Though he wore the humble robes of a monk, he had the bearing of a Greek nobleman.

An attendant interrupted to announce that the emperor was ready for them.

"Your ambassadors have arrived, I see!" declared Michael, greeting Photius and his guests. He peered intently at Constantine. "You have been told about this mission?"

"I have been told that you wish to build an alliance with the Khazars."

"Indeed. I have been in touch with the Kagan, leader of the Khazar people, and he has sent me an interesting reply."

"He has agreed to allow our visit?"

"More than that." Michael leaned back in his throne. "Explain, patriarch."

"Many of the Kagan's people are Jews," began Photius. "The nearby nations are Muslim. The Kagan is under increasing pressure to accept one of these as the official religion of his kingdom. But he appears to be a most reasonable man. He has asked the emperor to send a Christian teacher to debate with Jewish and Muslim representatives. He will choose a religion after he hears all the arguments."

The emperor broke in. "According to the patriarch, you are the only one capable of leading this mission, Constantine. Your brother has considerable diplomatic experience and will assist you."

Methodius nodded politely and remained silent.

"If you are successful in this debate, the two of you will lead a new missionary effort among the Khazar Slavs," said Photius, leaning forward with excitement. "God has given us a rare opportunity to declare his gospel to these people at their own request."

Constantine agreed. "My brother and I are honored to accept this task."

"I will send soldiers and servants to protect and assist you," said Michael. "You will travel by way of the Black Sea, and stop first in Cherson, on the Crimean Peninsula."

"Cherson!" Constantine looked at the emperor in surprise.

"There is much unrest in that area. You will gather military intelligence before finishing your journey north."

Constantine glanced from Methodius to Photius to Michael. "Emperor, may I make a request? Tradition says that Cherson is where the bones of the great bishop Clement of Rome are buried!"

The emperor tapped his fingers on his thigh. "You wish to search for his remains?"

"If you will grant us permission. It would be a remarkable discovery for the church."

"Very well. You may take an expedition while my military agents gather intelligence. But do not allow this quest to distract you from the debate with the Kagan," he growled. "An alliance with the Khazars is a top priority for the empire. At the patriarch's recommendation, I am trusting our security to you."

"It is an honor to serve God and the emperor."

Impatiently, Michael waved them out.

It took several weeks to prepare for their journey. As soon as they had gathered all the personnel and supplies they would need for several months away, the brothers sailed north across the Black Sea.

Constantine stood on the bow as they approached the port of Cherson. A light headwind had picked up overnight and now flung chilly foam in his face. Trade ships clogged the docks, rocking in the dark waters of the harbor as cargo was unloaded. He shielded his eyes and gazed up at the rows of sun-bleached houses ascending the peninsula above the shore.

Wrapping his robes tightly against the chill, Methodius joined him at the railing.

"Do you hear those sailors on the docks?" Constantine said to his brother. "There are at least three dialects I don't recognize."

"Looks like someone is expecting us." Methodius pointed to one of the easternmost docks.

Constantine saw a round man in purple robes at the head of a small crowd.

"Holy Constantine! Welcome!" The man hailed them with a wave as the sailors roped them to the dock.

They stepped off the ship and greeted their hosts.

"I am George, archbishop of Cherson." He bowed, and the welcome party with him followed suit. "You honor us with your visit. It is rare that we receive visitors from the Greek church this far north."

"We bring greetings from Patriarch Photius," said Constantine with a smile.

Methodius glanced curiously at an old man behind the archbishop. He appeared not to see the brothers, but was humming a familiar melody. "Is it tradition to greet your visitors with singing?"

"Oh," said George. "That is my cleric, John. He loves to sing hymns, and does so all day long! I don't even notice anymore. But, never mind that," said George, pushing through the crowd. "Come, we have prepared quarters for you."

They followed him into town, John humming quietly behind them.

The brothers tarried in Cherson for several weeks, visiting with George and preaching in the local church. While the emperor's agents gathered details about political and military concerns, Constantine and Methodius worked to learn the local Slav dialect.

"You are quick to speak our language!" said George with approval.

"It will be a great help in communicating the gospel here and further north in Khazar land."

When they told George of their plan to search for Clement's burial place, he eagerly assisted them.

"The relics of the second bishop of Rome would be a find indeed! You think they are here?"

"An early Christian legend says he was exiled here by Emperor Trajan and sentenced to hard labor in the mines. Trajan later ordered that he be executed by drowning."

George clapped. "You shall have whatever you need for the expedition. And be sure to take John! You will certainly want someone to lead worship when you find the holy site."

Methodius looked meaningfully at his brother, but Constantine accepted the archbishop's offer with a gracious smile.

It took only a few days to find the small inlet where rumors said a martyr was buried. They took a boat, leaving it on the shoal along the barren coast, and climbed toward the ruins of a tiny chapel. Constantine was the one who spotted the small stone marker.

"This is it!" he said. "Dig here. It is time we returned the great bishop's remains to his beloved Rome."

The box of bones was quickly uncovered. Constantine himself carried the box on his shoulders as they returned to Cherson. The brothers were so excited about their find that even the cleric's constant singing was forgotten.

George was overjoyed. "Notify the governor! We must declare a feast day to celebrate our good fortune."

They left the sacred relics in Cherson when they set off on the second half of their journey. George promised to take good care of them until they returned from the Kagan's debate.

The Khazar leader's residence was located on the western shores of the Caspian Sea. Constantine's delegation crossed the peninsula to the Maeotis Sea and boarded another ship, following the sea to the Don River and then to the Volga River. The Volga emptied into the Caspian Sea in the foothills of the Caucasus Mountains. The rounded spires of the Kagan's palace were visible from the shore.

Their arrival was expected, and an attendant immediately ushered them into the Kagan's court.

"Hello!" cried their host, rising from his seat with outstretched arms. He was tall, a bit older than they had expected, but his squared beard showed no gray. "I am honored to welcome you into my house. Your reputation as holy men has spread throughout my land."

"Thank you," said Constantine.

"I am told you have found the bones of one of your saints."

"The news has traveled fast. Clement was one of the first great Christian leaders."

"I am more curious than ever! Clearly you have the blessing of your god. And tonight you shall tell us about him. My Jewish and Muslim guests have already arrived. We shall feast and debate for many nights!" He shouted for his servants to attend to his visitors.

That evening they were shown into a great dining hall where many guests had already arrived. Some chatted in groups around the perimeter. Others had been seated at two broad tables spanning the length of the hall. Scarlet-clad dancers performed to the music of a dozen flutes. The room was warm, despite its great size, and heavy with the scent of perfume and rich food.

A servant met the brothers as they entered. "What is your rank, please? Everyone is seated according to title and nobility."

Constantine glanced at Methodius, his eyes twinkling mischievously. "My grandfather is very well known, and was once a close friend of the most powerful ruler in the world. But he chose to forsake his position and was banished. I have never been able to regain the noble position he once held."

"Who is this grandfather, and where was his noble residence?"

"His name was Adam, and he walked with God in the Garden of Eden."

"A clever answer!" cried the Kagan, clapping with approval. He had been watching them from his position at the center of the table. "These two will be seated near me, for I have many questions to ask of them."

They sat, and their host took great pleasure in introducing them to his other guests. The Jewish representative, a man called Isaac, was obviously an old friend of the Kagan's. He wore a black mantle across his shoulders, and had sharp but friendly eyes. Akmed, the Muslim debater, said nothing as the brothers were introduced, but acknowledged them with a regal nod of his turban. Constantine quickly forgot the names of the others as the Kagan pointed out dozens of distinguished guests around the room. Clearly, only the noblest of Khazar society had been invited to their leader's unusual feast.

An army of servants buzzed around the tables, setting steaming platters and bowls before the Kagan. When he nodded his approval, the dishes were distributed to the guests.

Constantine took a bite of the stewed meat in front of him. It was moist and pleasantly spicy.

The room grew quiet as the Kagan rapped his knuckles on the table. He sent away the entertainers with an impatient wave. "Tell me, honorable Constantine, why does your religion emphasize a book of divine writings? You memorize it and quote it, putting great value on the written word. But the traditional teachings of my people come from the heart instead of the head."

Constantine thought for a moment. "Suppose you met a naked man who boasted that he had many garments. Would you believe him?"

A chuckle ran around the room.

"Of course not," replied the Kagan with a hearty laugh. "If he has so many garments, why is he naked?"

"Exactly," said Constantine. "Christians do not just boast about our religion. We open the Scriptures and show you what our God says."

"A wise answer." The Kagan raised his mug. "Let us drink in the name of the One God who made all of creation."

"I drink in the name of the One God *and* his Word, Jesus," said Constantine. "It is through Jesus the Son and in the name of the life-giving Spirit that God created the world." He drained his glass.

The corners of their host's mouth twitched in puzzlement. "We both speak of the God of creation, but you glorify his son and spirit as though they are equal. Is there not only one God?"

"You are right that there is only one God, but he exists in three persons. We must honor all three equally, for the one who honors God, but does not honor his Son or his Spirit, does not honor him fully."

"You claim that Jesus is God's son," Isaac interjected. "But no one is worthy to even look upon God. How, therefore, can anyone give birth to him? How is it possible for a woman to contain God in her womb?"

"Did not God contain himself in a bush when he appeared to Moses?"

The Kagan smiled. "Another clever answer."

The debate continued long after they had finished the meal. The candles were burning low when the Kagan rose from the table. "The hour has grown late," he declared. "We shall continue tomorrow."

The next night they returned to the great hall. And the next night. And the night after that. Each evening, the Kagan asked questions as his guests debated which religion was true. Standing in the shadows along the walls, the nobles listened intently.

On the final night of feasting, the room was packed with observers, even more than had come on the other nights.

As soon as the meal was served, Akmed rose and gave a stately bow.

"Please explain," he said to Constantine, "why you do not follow Muhammad and his writings in the Qur'an. Does he not praise your Christ?"

"Yes, his writings praise Christ, but Muhammad calls himself the Prophet of God. The book of Daniel in the Bible says that Christ is the Prophet of God. Do we reject Daniel in favor of your prophet?"

"The Bible is an honorable book," answered Akmed, "but it is flawed. The word of Muhammad in the Qur'an is from God. It contains no error."

Isaac jumped to his feet. "Daniel wrote as he was directed by God's spirit. Anyone who teaches that Daniel's writings are flawed is a liar, and that includes Muhammad!"

The nobles burst into conversation, shouting out questions and insults.

"Quiet!" cried the Kagan. "Honorable Constantine, you may make a final statement."

Constantine got to his feet and addressed the whole room. "Brothers and fathers, friends and children! God has given me faith, without which no one can be saved."

Tears glimmered in his eyes as he gazed at those seated around him. His voice was low and intense.

"If you do not embrace Christ and receive baptism in the name of the Holy Trinity, you will be judged by the Ancient of Days, and he will find you wanting."

The room was silent. The Kagan rose.

"All of my invited guests have spoken. I have heard your many arguments, and it is time for me to decide which religion is true. You shall have my answer in the morning."

They rose early the next day and prepared for the journey back to Cherson.

"I will go down to the sea and make sure our supplies are loaded onto the ship," offered Methodius. "You will join me there once you've received word from the Kagan?"

Constantine nodded. But Methodius was stopped at the door by a servant. "The Kagan wishes to see you, please."

The brothers glanced at each other. "This is it," said Constantine. "We will soon know if our mission has been successful."

They followed the messenger to the gates of the palace. Hundreds of people had gathered there to see them off. A well-dressed man stopped the brothers as they passed. "The words you spoke yesterday have lodged in my heart," said the man. "My friends and I discussed your arguments last night after the feast was concluded. We want to learn more about your God and be baptized."

Constantine smiled. "That is wonderful, my friend. Praise be to God!"

The crowd parted to make way for the Kagan, who waved a letter in his hand. "I have written a message to your emperor. Allow me to read: *Honorable Michael, you have sent us holy men, who in word and deed have shown us that the Christian faith is holy. I am convinced it is the true faith. Any of my people who wish to do so shall be baptized.*"

The noble and his friends cheered.

"You will see that this letter is delivered to your emperor?"

"Of course." Constantine tucked the message safely into his belt.

The Kagan bowed low before the brothers. "The people of Khazar are friends of the empire. We are at your service, whenever you require it."

"You are most gracious. I'm sure the emperor will send you Christian teachers right away."

"Thank you, thank you. Now, please accept these gifts to your emperor."

He signaled to his servants, who brought forward crates of furs and mounds of spices and jewels.

"Oh, no," said Constantine, shaking his head. "The gospel is a free gift of God, and we did not bring it to exchange for earthly treasures."

"I mean no insult. I merely wish to demonstrate my appreciation to your emperor. Tell me what he would consider a worthy gift."

"You have Greek prisoners?"

The Kagan raised his eyebrows. "Of course. There are always border skirmishes."

"Then release them, and allow me to take them back to Constantinople. That will mean more to the emperor than your beautiful gifts."

"Done!"

By the end of the day, the brothers and the rest of their entourage, including 200 released captives, had cast off the Kagan's private docks on the Caspian Sea and set out for Cherson. They would preach there for a few more weeks while the emperor's agents finished their work, and then return to Constantinople.

Methodius and Constantine met on deck once the ship was underway.

"Now that the Khazars wish to follow Christ, they need a Bible in their language," said Constantine.

"So do the people of Cherson and the rest of the Crimean

Peninsula," agreed Methodius. "But none of the Slavic peoples have a written language."

"I know. But I've mastered their speech, and I think I can devise a written language so we can begin translating the Bible."

Methodius laughed. "Knowing you, you'll have the project finished before we reach Cherson!"

Constantine smiled. "Methodius, when I dedicated myself to the Lord's work at that monastery on Mount Olympus, I had no idea he would send me on such a mission."

"He used us to take the gospel to the Khazars *and* free our own people."

"And we've made an ally in protecting the empire against the Rus. Photius and the emperor will be pleased."

Methodius grinned. "I wish the cleric was here to sing!"

They stood together in silence as the ship moved north along the shore toward the mouth of the Volga River. The sun began to sink behind the mountains, and soon the domed towers of the Kagan's palace were just shadows in the darkening sky.

Constantine and Methodius soon returned to Slavic territory as missionaries. They developed a written Slavic language and translated the Bible so the people could read it for themselves. When Constantine died on February 14, 869, the Roman pope renamed him Cyril, and he has been known by that name ever since. Methodius died on the mission field on April 6, 885.

Emperor Michael was murdered by Caesar Basil, who banished Patriarch Photius from Constantinople.

Historians now believe that the bones the brothers discovered in Cherson did not belong to Bishop Clement of Rome, but were confused with those of another Christian named Clement who was martyred on the Crimean Peninsula. Clement of Rome's true remains have never been found.

Vladimir: If you know him, you too will rejoice

AUTUMN 968. KIEV, IN THE LAND OF RUS (NOW RUSSIA).

THE PRIEST STOOD at the door to the chamber, peering anxiously down the corridor. It was deserted. Only a few servants remained in the palace, and the priest had sent them scurrying to pack supplies as soon as his messenger had arrived. Now it was time to execute the final stage of their plan.

"Please, Helen," he urged. "The messenger has arrived. There isn't much time, princess."

"I'm ready." The woman brushed a lock of silver-streaked hair from her strong forehead and put comforting arms around the two boys clinging to her skirts.

A third boy, smaller than the other two, stood apart from them. He glared at the priest. Like his brothers, the boy's head was shaved except for a ponytail on the left side, identifying him with his father's clan. "Her name is Olga!" he said defiantly.

The priest forced a tolerant smile. "Of course, Prince Vladimir. But Helen is her Christian name, the one she chose at her baptism."

"Her name is Olga!" insisted Vladimir, his shoulders stiffening.

The woman turned to the child and put a gentle hand on his smooth head. The corners of her dark eyes crinkled in a smile. "Alright," she agreed. "How can I refuse such a smart and handsome young man?"

She drew the boys to her and looked up at the priest. "My grandson and my people call me Olga. You may do so as well."

"As you wish," replied the priest with a nod. "But we must go now or our messenger will have journeyed in vain."

"Follow him, boys."

They hurried into the corridor, following it as it curved away from the inner chambers of the palace. Vladimir elbowed his brother Yaropolk and edged closer to Olga.

"You should treat our grandmother better," said Yaropolk. "Her Christian religion is ancient."

Vladimir shoved him, and Yaropolk tripped. The exasperated priest scooped up the boy and kept moving. As they neared the outer court, the roar outside the gates grew louder. Four soldiers met them in the courtyard, bowing until Olga extended her hand.

"What is the situation?"

"Our plan worked," said the captain. "Our messenger ran through the Pecheneg army with a bridle, asking if anyone had seen his horse. They thought he was one of theirs and just laughed at him. When he reached the Dnieper River, he jumped in and swam to the other side. He got the message to Prince Svyatoslav that Kiev is under siege."

Olga breathed a sigh of relief. "Thank God! My son will return soon with the armies of Rus and rescue our starving city!"

"Yes, but we can't take any chances," said the priest. "You and the princes must leave tonight."

"General Pretich will meet us at the Dnieper," said the captain.

"But we have to go now while it is dark."

Olga threw back her shoulders. "Lead the way."

They slipped out into the darkness and followed the soldiers. The princess slowed her pace, taking Vladimir by the arm.

"Anything can happen in the next few hours, Vladimir, so listen carefully to me," she said. "I have learned to know God, and am glad for it. If you know him, you too will rejoice."

He scowled at her. "My father's gods are my gods."

"You must hear me," his grandmother insisted. "When I was a young girl in Pskov, I heard of the great missionaries Constantine and Methodius, and I, too, rejected their religion. But now that I have visited Constantinople and worshiped the Creator God in his beautiful churches, I know that I was a fool."

Vladimir wrenched himself out of her grip. "I am no fool! I will reign in my father's place one day with the blessing of our gods." The tassels on his silk tunic rustled as he strode ahead of her.

She squeezed her eyes shut and prayed. *O God, save him from himself. Use him to declare your glory to the people of Rus.*

The priest had stopped ahead of them and was anxiously waving at her to hurry. Glancing behind her at the palace's dark profile against the starless sky, she picked up her skirts and rushed to catch up with the soldiers.

Twenty winters passed.

A well-dressed Byzantine ambassador, followed by several attendants, was escorted to a chamber deep inside the palace of Kiev. The guards did not announce him, but took up positions inside the door.

Three men were waiting for him at a table. The one in the center had a long ponytail on the left side of his otherwise shaved head. "I'm Vladimir," he said. "You are Basil's messenger?"

The Greek nodded. "My name is James."

"Sit."

James took an empty place at the table. His companions remained standing behind him.

Vladimir gestured to the older man seated at his left. "Dobrynya, my political advisor."

Dobrynya nodded, but didn't smile. James returned the greeting warily.

"And this is General Wolf's Tail, my military advisor," continued the prince.

James blinked. "How does a man get the name of a soulless animal?"

The general crossed his arms over his tattered, animal-hide vest and glared at him from half-lowered eyelids.

Vladimir grinned. "Those who meet him in battle understand!"

Wolf's Tail growled suddenly in amusement and bared his teeth. Startled, James dropped his gaze to the rough-hewn tabletop. He noticed, below it, a thick rug covering the floor with a dark pattern of interlocking squares.

"Satisfy my curiosity, Greek," said Vladimir. "Why did Basil send you all the way from Constantinople? Is he afraid I will conquer his city? Perhaps he wants to surrender now!"

James stared at the prince, unsure of his response. He couldn't imagine the Byzantine emperor receiving a visiting dignitary in such a manner.

Vladimir broke into a deep belly laugh, echoed by Dobrynya. Wolf's Tail didn't flinch.

"I'm not serious, of course," said Vladimir, leaning across the table. "Just having a little fun at your expense."

James offered a tentative smile.

The prince frowned back. "You are here with a message, aren't you? I want to know why Constantinople sends messengers all the way to Kiev."

"Of course," stammered James. "I assure you, prince, the emperor prefers to be your friend, not your ruler."

"A preference I am inclined to indulge!"

"Emperor Basil seeks a partnership."

Vladimir leaned back on his bench and stretched his neck until it cracked. The sound was startling in the quiet chamber.

James placed his hands on the table in front of him. "Since your brother Yaropolk's mysterious death, you have been sole ruler of Rus. You have expanded your father's territories far beyond their original borders. And you have restored the worship of your ancestors, even convincing your people to sacrifice their children in the flames! You are obviously a very powerful man."

"None of this is news to me, Greek. What is your point?"

"Bardas Phokas, in Anatolia, is marching on Constantinople even as we speak. Emperor Basil believes Phokas is a threat to us and to you."

Wolf's Tail snorted. "To *you*. Not to us."

"Perhaps not yet," retorted James, avoiding the general's hostile gaze and speaking directly to Vladimir. "But eventually Phokas will become a menace to Kiev as well. Before that happens, Emperor Basil appeals to you to help your friends in Constantinople."

"What's in it for me?" demanded the prince.

"Stability in the region, for one. Enlarging your territory has spread your power thin. Your recent struggle to control the Bulgars proves that. If you conquer any more cities, you will run out of men and supplies to defend yourself."

Vladimir shifted uncomfortably. The Greek was right. He would not be able to maintain his power for long without an alliance with Constantinople, but he was not about to admit such a weakness. He shrugged. "What else?"

"As a token of his appreciation, Emperor Basil offers his sister to become your wife."

"Ha!" barked Wolf's Tail. "She has donkey ears or a pig's snout? Basil can find no one else willing to take her?"

James raised his chin and glared at the general with blazing eyes. "Princess Anna is of the highest royal standards! She was raised in purple with her brother, and is beloved of the empire. No man fortunate to have seen her would say such a thing!"

Vladimir laughed and bowed mockingly. "You must forgive Wolf's Tail. He is a barbarian with no appreciation for beauty."

James frowned and said nothing. With care, he took a small package from one of the attendants behind him and placed it in the middle of the table.

Vladimir snatched it and unwrapped the fabric covering. It was a miniature portrait of a woman with large eyes and shining hair curled around a delicate face.

He smiled and tucked the portrait into his vest. "I'm listening."

"A marriage to the princess would offer strong political ties not only with Constantinople, but with all of our allies," said James. He made a face as though his words tasted bitter.

Dobrynya spoke for the first time. "It is well-known that the Greeks do not allow their women to marry foreigners."

"That is nearly true," admitted James, "but not quite. It is not foreigners that we object to, but their pagan religions. Christians do not marry pagans." He turned to the prince. "If you wish to marry Princess Anna, you must first accept Christianity."

"Of course!" Vladimir threw up his hands and leaned back again, shifting his gaze to the ceiling. *There is no escaping the religion of my grandmother*, he thought. Every day he remembered the night they had escaped from the besieged Kiev, and how beautiful and earnest she had looked as she urged him to turn to Christianity. He loved her fiercely, but her approval was not worth rejecting the ancient gods and jeopardizing his power.

Vladimir's voice was low. "The guards will provide whatever

you need. You will be notified of my decision."

James was happy to leave them, his companions following in his hasty footsteps.

"You can't forsake our gods," grunted Wolf's Tail. "They give us protection and prosperity."

"Wolf's Tail is wise in military matters, but not politics," said Dobrynya. "Our nation is strong, but it could be stronger with the emperor's sister as your wife. Surely the gods wish that."

The general glowered at the old man. "He already has more wives than I can count on one hand!"

Vladimir grinned. "Is it my fault that there are so many beautiful women in my kingdom?"

Wolf's Tail spat on the floor.

"The Greek princess is more than just another wife," said Dobrynya. "Her presence here creates a permanent bond between our peoples. She ensures a profitable alliance."

"Only if he abandons our ancient religions for this ridiculous Greek myth! It is too high a price for one more specimen in his collection!" Wolf's Tail spat again.

Dobrynya turned away in disgust. "Vladimir, Christianity is the religion of your grandmother. She was no fool! And plenty of others in Kiev followed her beliefs after she spoke of her visit to Constantinople. We must accept the fact that the religions of Rus have put us at a political disadvantage in our relations with the Greeks. It is time to change that."

The prince rose and began to pace, his back to his advisors. "Over the last few years," he said, "our borders have expanded rapidly. The Muslims have tried to convince me to accept their religion. The Khazars sent Jewish teachers. The Latin Christians in Germany sent their priests. And now the Greeks! Everyone wants Rus to forsake the old gods!"

Dobrynya spoke quietly but firmly. "My prince, our religion is a thing of the past. We must consider our future."

"Of course I'm thinking of our future! I sent our people to Constantinople to see what the Greeks were talking about."

"And they were impressed," reminded Dobrynya. "Remember what they said? They didn't know if they were in heaven or on earth, because the churches were so beautiful. They were convinced that God dwells there."

Vladimir ran a hand over his smooth head. "So be it," he said. "An alliance is good for our future, and another woman is good for me. I will agree to Basil's proposal."

The general pounded the table with his fist. "The gods of Rus— ."

"Enough!" shouted Vladimir. "I have made my decision, and you, general, will lead the army."

With a growl, Wolf's Tail smashed his stool against the wall and stomped out.

With the assistance of Vladimir's army, Basil successfully defeated Phokas' advance. All of Kiev celebrated as Wolf's Tail and his men returned, but Vladimir was furious to discover that Princess Anna was not with them.

"Where is she?" he demanded, when the general arrived with his report.

"I told you the Greeks could not be trusted!"

"Basil refuses to keep his end of our agreement?"

The general handed him a letter marked with Basil's imperial seal. "She does not wish to leave her people."

"It is not her decision!"

"Obviously Basil is weak and allows a woman to dictate to him!"

Vladimir flung the letter to the ground and crushed it under his boots. "If Basil will not give me his sister, then I will take another prize. Prepare to attack the city of Cherson!"

"Why Cherson?"

"Why not? It is a valuable port city close to my territory, and the Greeks have controlled it far too long. I will show Basil what happens when he betrays the Great Prince of Kiev!"

Following the custom of his father, he sent a messenger ahead to warn them of his approach. "Tell them if they refuse to surrender, I will lay siege to the city until they starve!"

Vladimir took shifts manning the oars with his men as they sailed down the Dnieper. They halted on the harbor side of the city.

"Begin constructing earthworks," ordered the prince. "Anyone who tries to get in or out of the city will have to climb the mounds, making himself an excellent target for our archers. No food or supplies will make it through."

"Cherson will fall in a matter of days," declared Wolf's Tail. "You have only enough time to sacrifice to the gods."

"Send a message to Constantinople," replied Vladimir. "Tell Basil if he will not give me the princess, I will take his precious city. And if he continues to refuse, I will take Constantinople, too."

The prince worked alongside his army. Within days, they had constructed a tall mound of dirt around the perimeter of the city.

"I am too old for this digging," grumbled Wolf's Tail, rubbing his sore shoulders as they prepared to sleep on the sixth night. "But the barrier is now complete." He nodded toward the north, where a line of flickering torches reassured him that Vladimir's watchful archers were at their posts.

"Now we wait for them to surrender." The prince stretched out on a blanket with his saddle under his head, and was soon snoring confidently.

The early morning light revealed a strange gap in the earthworks.

"What is this?" demanded Vladimir.

"I don't know," said the general. "The men were at their posts all night and saw no one, but somehow the soil was removed."

"Where is the missing dirt?"

"We can't find it, sir. It's just gone."

"Find it!" ordered the prince.

The men filled in the missing section of the earthworks. Vladimir himself stood watch that night, but all was quiet.

In the morning, the soil in another location was gone.

Vladimir and Wolf's Tail rode north to a hilly area overlooking the city.

"What's your theory?" asked the prince. "Do we have a ghost? Or do the citizens of Cherson have a god of dirt?"

The general grunted. "A new god to add to the hillside at Kiev."

Vladimir squinted at the city and frowned. "Do you see that, just inside the wall, near the church? I don't remember seeing a hill there."

Wolf's Tail shaded his eyes. "That is our earthworks!"

"They're carting the dirt into the city at night! By creating gaps in the barriers, they can slip out for supplies without being seen."

"Clever. There must be holes in the city walls, because we know the gates are sealed."

"Inspect the walls," ordered Vladimir. "Post guards at the openings just outside of a bow-shot. Now that we know where to look, we'll keep them from getting out."

The earthworks were untouched that night.

"It worked," declared the general. "But they still refuse to surrender."

"When they're hungry enough, they'll surrender. We'll wait!"

Weeks passed. There was no reply from Basil, and Cherson showed no signs of surrender.

It was a hot afternoon, and Vladimir stood in the shade of a tree on the hillside with several of his men.

"Why haven't they run out of water yet?"

"I can answer that," called Wolf's Tail, riding up on his horse. He had an arrow in his left hand and a crumpled message in his right.

"What is this?"

"The arrow was shot over the city wall with the message attached. It claims to be from a man inside the city named Anastasius. Apparently, he wants to end the siege."

"Finally, a traitor! If he survives the attack, reward him."

"Their water supply is no longer a secret. The note details the position of pipes running underground from a spring into the city. That's how they have withstood our siege for so long."

"Cut off the water," ordered Vladimir. "Now."

They soon found the natural spring in a rocky area north of the city. Cool water bubbled up in a series of connecting pools, nearly hidden by ferns and shrubs flourishing in the moist soil.

"Dig," the general shouted at his men. "The pipes are under here somewhere."

They dug until the sun went down. Wolf's Tail sent for torches, and ordered the men to keep digging.

"I've got something!" came a shout.

Vladimir snatched up a torch and followed the general. One of the men stood in a hole slowly filling with water. "I think I cracked the pipe."

"Destroy it!" shouted Vladimir.

As soon as the people of Cherson discovered their water was gone, they surrendered. Vladimir and his men marched into the hungry city.

"Send word to Constantinople," said the prince. "Tell Basil I have captured his glorious city, and I am going to do the same to Constantinople if he does not deliver the princess."

Wolf's Tail nodded.

"And then get these people some food."

"Sir?"

"I didn't come to destroy their city. I just came for my bride."

They found a comfortable house to inhabit while the general's messengers made their way to Constantinople. A ship arrived a week later with a reply from the emperor.

"Anna has agreed to marry you," declared the messenger, "*if* you will be baptized and promote Christianity in Rus."

"Basil is still making demands?" cried Wolf's Tail. "We'll take his capital anyway!"

Vladimir shook his head. "It will take a substantial force to capture Constantinople. The troops in Kiev would be depleted, and my enemies will take advantage of the opportunity."

"I won't take orders from a Greek!"

Vladimir swung around. "You'll take orders from me. Dobrynya is right. We need this alliance."

"The cost of such an alliance is too high. You're willing to forsake the gods of Kiev for a woman?"

The prince shrugged. "If she brings her god to Kiev, he can look out for us."

"He better! Once you reject the gods of our forefathers, our people will be left unprotected."

"He'll have the assistance of my army." He softened. "The Christian god was good enough for my grandmother."

"What does a woman know about religion?"

He shot Wolf's Tail a warning look. "She was a wise ruler, even if she was a woman. No one will speak ill of her." *She was always at peace, even when she was surrounded by war,* he remembered. She had insisted that he would rejoice if he met her god.

"Kiev and Constantinople shall become brothers," Vladimir declared.

"Ah, what a comfort to Constantinople," said Wolf's Tail. "Hopefully Basil has forgotten that you ordered your brother

Yaropolk's assassination and took his wife."

"You speak too freely, general."

Wolf's Tail grunted, but said no more.

"Deliver a message to Basil," said the prince. "Tell him, *I have learned about your religion from my grandmother. If it will bring Kiev and Constantinople closer as allies, I will be baptized as a Christian.*"

The general hesitated.

"Go!" Vladimir barked. "And tell him I'm waiting for my wife!"

Vladimir was baptized in Cherson. After his marriage to Anna, he returned the city to Basil as a groom's gift. Though he appears to have converted to Christianity for purely political reasons, history records that Vladimir took his vows seriously. He tore down the idols in Kiev, founded churches throughout Rus, and built schools to teach his people how to read the Bible.

When Vladimir died in 1015, his kingdom was divided among his three sons. Following his father's example, Svyatopolk murdered his brothers Boris and Gleb and seized their territories. But Christianity had taken root in Rus and became the dominant religion of the next ten centuries.

A Divided Church: The Great Schism of 1054

SINCE THE EARLY centuries of the church, Christians in the western world (centered in Rome, Italy) and Christians in the eastern world (centered in Constantinople, Byzantium) had many differences. It was natural that as Christianity spread into lands outside the Roman Empire, Christians were introduced to new cultures. Most of the time, new believers in these regions continued to follow local customs. Even though Latin, the language of Rome, was used in church services, the people in these regions rarely used it in everyday life. In the eastern regions, Greek remained the common language. People often mistrust others who don't share their language or customs.

Sometimes the differences between east and west were about *doctrine*, or church teachings. One example is the *Nicene Creed*, a statement written at the Council of Nicea to define the church's teachings about the Trinity. The western church added a line to explain that teaching better, but the eastern church believed it corrupted the teaching instead. Another example is the question of whether clerics could be married. In the west, clerics had to vow to remain single. But in the east they were allowed to marry. So western clerics believed the eastern ones were less dedicated to the church, and eastern clerics believed the western ones were too strict.

Eastern Christians decorated churches with images of saints and even prayed to them. They said that as the saints were with God in heaven, they could speak to God on behalf of the living. They argued that just as Old Testament believers carved images of angels on the Ark of the Covenant, they should use sculptures and paintings of saints in worship. But the west said these were sinful idols. From Rome, the pope commanded the eastern church to stop honoring saint's images. But the east resisted.

Since the eastern congregations were so far away from Rome, they set up local leaders. At first there were *patriarchs*, or bishops, of equal authority in many eastern cities. But the eastern emperor lived in the city of Constantinople and with his support the patriarch of Constantinople became the final authority in the eastern church. When disagreements arose between east and west, the patriarch began to challenge the decisions of the pope.

The divide continued to grow. Finally, Pope Leo IX demanded that Patriarch Michael Caerularius submit to the authority of Rome. Patriarch Michael refused. For several years the two sides argued. Then the patriarch closed all the Latin churches in Constantinople. Furious, Pope Leo sent representatives to Constantinople on July 16, 1054 to *excommunicate* (or put out of the church) the patriarch. In response, Patriarch Michael excommunicated the pope's messengers.

Over the next several centuries, many attempts were made to reunite the east and west, including the Second Council of Lyons in 1274 and the Council of Florence in 1439. But in 1453, Muslim armies captured Constantinople. The rift was complete.

Followers of the eastern tradition became known as *Eastern*

Orthodox. Followers of the western tradition were known as *Roman Catholic*.

Five hundred years later, during the *Protestant Reformation*, the western tradition divided again—but that event deserves its own account.

Anselm of Canterbury: May God So Reign in Your Heart

AUGUST 2, 1100. ENGLAND.

OVERNIGHT, A GENTLE rain had moved through the English countryside, but by sunrise the sky was clear and fresh. It was a perfect morning for a hunting expedition. The king's party, bows at the ready, urged their horses through the New Forest.

William the Conqueror, king of Normandy, had invaded England in 1066. When he died, he had left the duchy of Normandy to his son Robert, and England to his son William Rufus. The third son, Henry, had received only 5,000 pounds of silver. It was this third son and the King of England, William Rufus, who now scouted the forest.

A flash of brown crossed the path, plunging into the undergrowth on the other side. "This way!" shouted one of the hunters, drawing a bow.

They plowed into the brush after the deer, trampling the tall grasses under galloping hooves.

"She must have gone into that stand of trees."

"We'll flush her out," cried the king, turning in his saddle to face his companions.

"Henry, take the others and cut over to the far side of the field. Walter and I will follow her into the trees."

"As you wish," nodded Henry, but he turned with a wink to the king's escort. "Walter, keep an eye on my brother. The king is not as keen with a bow as he thinks he is!"

"I am far more skilled than you!" laughed King William Rufus. "And even if I wasn't, who's going to stop me from taking credit for your shot?" He urged his horse forward, and disappeared into the trees with Walter at his heels.

The rest of the party skirted the woods, following Prince Henry toward the other side. They were only halfway there when they heard the zinging of arrows and Walter's shouts.

"Come quickly!" cried Walter. "Hurry!"

They rushed into the trees. Lying where he had fallen from his horse was the king. A scarlet stain was spreading out from an arrow buried deep in his chest.

"My brother!" shouted Henry, leaping off his horse. "What happened?"

Walter threw himself across the king's feet, weeping. "We didn't coordinate our approach," he cried. "The deer ran out right in front of us, and we both drew our bows. But the king! He, he wasn't paying attention. He rode directly into the path of my arrow!"

The men gathered around as Henry took his brother's face in his hands. "The king is dead," he declared quietly. "Take him home."

His companions carried the king's body to his horse.

Walter remained on his knees. "My lord, I beg you to forgive your servant. Your brother's death was an accident."

"Do not blame yourself," said Henry, shrugging and snatching up the king's bow. "He was never an able hunter. It was bound to happen."

"Oh, you are most gracious, my lord. Or should I say, my king?"

Henry smiled and urged his horse into a gallop. He flew across the fields toward Salisbury, leaving his companions to follow slowly behind, bearing their fallen king back to his people.

Several weeks later, a group of clerics gathered at a table in a house in la Chaise-Dieu, France.

"We are grateful for your hospitality, Archbishop Anselm," said one of the visitors. "We have been anxious to see how you have fared since you've been away from England."

"Time passes quickly when I am writing," replied their host.

"I read your books as fast as you write them. They have opened the Scriptures to me in ways I never imagined."

The archbishop smiled. "How kind of you to say, Gundulf."

"Your method of proving God's existence is a challenge to any atheist."

"It is a matter of simple logic," replied Anselm. "If we can imagine a perfect God, then he must exist. If he doesn't exist, he is less than perfect, and therefore cannot be God."

Bishop Gundulf chuckled. "It is a puzzle to be contemplated on sleepless nights!"

The conversation was disrupted by a knock at the door. A man writing quietly at a nearby table set down his quill and answered it.

Two monks stood on the doorstep.

"We have an urgent message for Archbishop Anselm," said one.

"I am Eadmer, the archbishop's personal assistant. What is the message?"

"King William Rufus is dead!" the man blurted.

"What?"

"His Excellency was killed in a hunting accident. Henry is now on the throne!"

Eadmer quickly ushered the monks inside. Everyone at the

table had heard their startling announcement.

"If Rufus is dead, your exile is over," said Gundulf, turning to Anselm. "You can return to England now."

"A bittersweet victory!" declared the archbishop. "Rufus and I were a young bull and an old sheep yoked to the same plow. We never saw eye to eye about matters of the church. I had hoped he would eventually change his mind." His shoulders drooped. "Now we will never reconcile."

"Yes, but Canterbury can receive back her archbishop."

Anselm sighed. He was tonsured, like all monks, and sometimes the shaved part of his head itched. He scratched it. "Exile has been a blessing in disguise. If I return to my duties in England, it will take far longer to finish my book on the Holy Spirit. Excuse me, friends." He rose suddenly and withdrew to the back of the house.

"Was it really an accident?" said Gundulf. "Everyone knows Henry has had designs on the crown for years."

The monks exchanged glances. "I heard that the man whose arrow killed Rufus just received a large estate from Henry."

The clerics broke into a flurry of whispers.

"With their brother Duke Robert away fighting in the Crusade, it was a good opportunity for Henry to take Rufus's place as king."

"Sssh! That kind of talk will get you exiled, or worse."

"But Robert is returning to Normandy from the Crusade. He has a new wife and great riches, and commands an entire army of knights! It is rumored that he has the power to reunite England and Normandy. Surely many of the nobles would support his claim to the throne."

"Perhaps. But England is tired of war. The nobles may prefer Henry to the tumult of another battle for power."

They grew quiet. After a thoughtful silence, Gundulf said, "The archbishop seemed to take the news rather harder than I expected."

"He's a complicated man," replied Eadmer. "And at his age, such news is a bit of a shock."

"He's not happy about returning to Canterbury."

"He never wanted to be archbishop, you know. He was content as abbot of the monastery at Bec after Lanfranc left to become archbishop."

"How exactly did Anselm receive the archbishopric anyway? The position had been vacant for several years after Lanfranc's death."

Eadmer leaned back in his chair. "King William Rufus chose not to replace Lanfranc, so he could use the profits from the archbishop's estates to fund his army. But the king became ill and soon feared he was dying. His advisors said God was punishing him for stealing from the church."

"He was!" said one of the clerics.

"Careful, son," said Bishop Gundulf. "Let Eadmer finish."

"Rufus decided to appoint a new archbishop immediately. At his insistence, the bishops of Canterbury invited Anselm to the king's bedside, supposedly to offer his personal counsel. Anselm believed the king was dying and rushed to Canterbury to pray with him. But when he arrived, Anselm noticed the archbishop's staff in the king's hand. He began to back away, but the king insisted. Anselm asked the pope to release him from the position, but the pope was pleased with the king's choice and refused to grant his request."

Gundulf nodded. "And then Rufus recovered from his illness."

"Yes, but Anselm's relationship with the king did not improve," Eadmer explained. "Rufus had given much of the church's lands to other vassals. Anselm insisted that the estates belonged to the church and were his right to oversee. Only after long disagreement did the king return the land. When Anselm asked the king for permission to travel to Rome to visit the new pope, Rufus refused. Anselm persisted. Finally the king granted him safe passage. But as soon as Anselm left, Rufus confiscated all of the church lands again. Anselm was forced to remain outside England."

"But now that Rufus is gone, certainly the archbishop will return."

"I will not be surprised if Henry sends an invitation immediately," declared Eadmer.

The message arrived a few weeks later. The archbishop's lands had been restored.

Anselm and Eadmer returned to England within the month. In spite of their anxiety about the new king, they found themselves smiling as the carriage whirled passed the tidy English farms. The archbishopric of Canterbury was an enormous estate on the mouth of the river Stour. Surrounded by villages and fields, the heart of the estate was Canterbury Cathedral and, nearby, the archbishop's private residence.

"I pray that I can carry on my duties in peace this time," Anselm said as he set foot on his own soil for the first time in several years.

Within days the archbishop was called to an audience with Henry. He went immediately to Salisbury. Proudly displayed inside the court was the coat of arms of William the Conqueror, Henry's father. But the banners representing the king's house were brand new.

Henry, wearing a bright blue brocade and his brother's crown, was deep in conversation with several courtiers. He smiled when Anselm was announced and waved them away, rising to greet his distinguished guest. "Welcome back, archbishop."

"Thank you, sire," replied Anselm. "I was grateful to receive your invitation to return. It is a proper beginning to your reign to promote the unity of Christ's church."

"That is, of course, why I recalled you. I intend to fulfill my kingly duties to the church."

"There is much to be done after these years of neglect."

"And I will defer to your wisdom in those matters. But I have two immediate items of business."

Anselm hesitated. He had an unpleasant feeling in the pit of his stomach.

"Your position as lord of the church's estates in Canterbury obligates you to the same responsibilities as other nobles. Before I can receive you back into royal favor, you must pay homage to your new king." Henry shrugged. "I cannot make exceptions if I am to retain the nobles' loyalty. I'm sure you can understand why that is a priority for me right now."

It was a conversation like this with William that led to my exile, Anselm thought. "And the second matter of business, sire?"

"You have been gone a long time, archbishop. I have appointed two new abbots and I need you to receive them into the church."

Anselm sighed. "With respect, sire, I'm afraid I cannot comply with your wishes."

Henry turned an unsmiling face on his guest. "These are simply standard procedures. You've done this before."

The archbishop looked away.

"You don't trust my judgment!" declared Henry with a sarcastic laugh. "You think I murdered my brother and my heart is too black to delve into sacred matters. Well, I assure you the new abbots are faithful churchmen. Actually, they are friends of yours."

"I have no idea what color your heart is, sire, and I shall not presume to suggest that His Excellency King William Rufus died of anything other than an unfortunate accident. But that is beside the point." Anselm shook his head. "While I was away from Canterbury, I attended a council in Rome. The church declared that investiture of clergy can be performed only by ordained bishops. Any lay person, no matter how high ranking, who takes it upon himself to appoint clergy, and any clergy who receive the one improperly invested, are to be disciplined by the church."

"That's ridiculous!"

"The council reached the same decision about clergy paying homage."

"I am king of this land!" cried Henry. "Homage and investiture are my kingly rights, just as they were the rights of my brother and my father."

Anselm was silent.

"Are you refusing to comply with my wishes?" the king demanded angrily.

"It is not my choice to either refuse or comply," said Anselm. "It is the decision of the church. The council's authority is greater than the wishes of any man, whether archbishop or king."

Henry clenched his fists and turned away. After a moment, he turned back with a calmer expression. "Frankly, I need the church's support during this time of transition. I will abide by the decisions of the council for now, but I suggest you give this more thought."

"Sire—."

"Enough business! It is time to introduce you to your soon-to-be queen." The king clapped his hands and called for his chamberlain. "I believe you have heard of Princess Matilda."

Anselm's jaw dropped. "The daughter of Malcolm, King of Scotland?"

"Don't look so shocked. It is a suitable marriage. She has royal blood, and an alliance with Scotland may prove to be an advantage."

"But Matilda has taken the monastic veil! She is a sister of the cloister at Wilton!"

Henry laughed. "You *do* believe I have a black heart! She is not a nun. She merely lived at the cloister for a time. We are to be married in a matter of days."

The princess was ushered in. She curtseyed and took the hand Henry offered her, but she avoided Anselm's gaze. The king frowned at them. "I have taken enough of your time, archbishop. I trust you will have reconsidered your position by our next meeting."

Anselm was escorted outside. A dozen knights nodded with respect as he passed. Eadmer had been waiting at the carriage, and now helped Anselm climb inside.

"Wait!"

Anselm looked down to see the princess hurrying toward him, her wide silk skirts swishing along the cobblestones.

"Please, archbishop. A word?"

Eadmer raised an eyebrow, but remained in his seat as Anselm stepped out of the carriage again. She grasped his arm in both hands and looked at him with pleading eyes. "Please archbishop. Do not condemn me for marrying Henry."

His reply was gentle but firm. "Do your monastic vows mean nothing to you, daughter?"

"My father sent me to Wilton with my Aunt Christina just to keep me out of his hair."

"He intended for you a life in the cloister."

She shook her head, the shining ringlets across her forehead bouncing. "He led everyone to believe that, especially after my engagement to Lord Richmond fell through. I know you wrote to the bishop of Salisbury about me then, worried that I was running away from the church. But the truth is that my father planned a noble marriage for me all along."

"A man or woman who has voluntarily taken a monastic vow must never abandon it."

"You know I have no choice in this matter. My father has arranged everything with Henry, and I am an obedient daughter. Surely God honors such obedience."

He frowned. "This matter is not my concern. I have just returned to England and I am already at odds with Henry!" He looked into her earnest face and sighed. "Seek the counsel of your chaplain,

Matilda. I will pray for you."

She squeezed his arm, still clutched in her small hands. "Will you write to me after the wedding? I can ask for no greater honor than to receive your letters."

"It is the least I can offer the future Queen of England." He gently released himself from her grip and turned back to the open carriage. "God be with you."

The horses jerked into motion as soon as he was safely inside. Eadmer watched the princess through the window until they pulled away from the tree-lined drive, and then turned to Anselm. The archbishop was scowling at him.

"My first week back in England, and already everything is complicated," said Anselm. "I made a disturbing discovery yesterday."

"About the king?"

"No, about my assistant."

Eadmer looked at him, startled.

"You've been keeping notes about my actions and things I've said," continued Anselm. "Why?"

"I'm just recording the details for the sake of history, like I did in my book about the life of Saint Wilfrid."

"I have enough to think about without worrying what history will say of me. I want you to burn your notes."

"But, master!"

"Destroy them, Eadmer. You have more important tasks to do."

"Yes, master."

The archbishop closed his eyes, as though he would nap. They said nothing more for the rest of the ride.

Eadmer burned his candle until late into the night. After hours of leaning over his desk, he rose and regretfully tossed a manuscript into his fireplace. The flames had gone out but the coals were hot, and the paper began to blacken and curl. With a small shovel, he picked out the charred remains and dropped them into a bin.

I have obeyed my master and destroyed the manuscript he found, Eadmer told himself. *And now I must sleep before he asks why I have been up all night*.

He blew out his candle and stretched out under a blanket. Below him, in the darkness under the straw mattress, was a stack of fresh pages, the ink still sticky. Across the top page, in his neat hand, was a simple headline: *Life of Anselm*.

The following months were difficult. Daily services were re-established at Canterbury Cathedral. Anselm had time to write only in the evenings, and dedicated himself to finishing his books. Eadmer helped Anselm with a growing amount of correspondence. Occasionally, one was addressed to the queen.

Henry's marriage caused a stir throughout the country, but the alliance with Scotland had been a shrewd decision. The nobles began to show less support for Robert. Henry continued to add to his army as hundreds of knights returned from the Crusade. The king regularly summoned Anselm to Salisbury, pressuring him to consecrate the new abbots and pay homage.

"Don't forget that I welcomed you back to England, archbishop," Henry declared.

"Yes, and I am thankful you did, but it was your Christian duty."

"I also restored to you the church lands my brother confiscated."

"Yes," agreed Anselm, "but, again, that was your Christian duty."

Henry slammed the table with his fist. "I'm sick of these overbearing church procedures! Know this: anyone who tries to take away the king's rights is the king's enemy!"

Anselm raised his eyebrows at Henry's outburst. The king paused and collected his temper.

"I am a loyal subject of the king," Anselm insisted quietly. "It is not my wish to take away your rights, sire, but even if it meant saving your life, I cannot and will not violate the commands of our church."

Henry leaned forward and spoke in a more conciliatory tone. "Then go to Rome and speak to the pope on my behalf."

Anselm blinked. "If you thought you could change the pope's mind, why have you not sent someone already?"

"I had hoped we could work this out without bothering the Holy Father. But the dignity of my office as king is founded on the rights of investiture and homage. To lose them is a disgrace."

"You would send an old man all the way to Rome?"

"You are the only one who can explain our disagreement to the pope."

Anselm sighed. "If it is the king's command, I will go, for the sake of the church of England."

"I hope you will not be offended if I also send a lawyer to be sure my rights are accurately represented."

"I assume you mean Lord William of Warelwast."

Henry smiled and rose in dismissal. "I commend you on your political awareness. William is a loyal friend. I am sure the two of you will have a profitable discussion in Rome."

Eadmer accompanied his master on the long journey to Rome. Anselm tired easily and they had to make several stops along the way. By the time they arrived, months later, Warelwast was already there, and had met privately with various members of the Roman council.

Pope Paschal welcomed his guest into Saint Peter's Basilica. The council of bishops, eager to hear their arguments, sat in neat rows facing the pope. Anselm and Eadmer were directed to seats on the right of the room, opposite Warelwast.

"For what reason does the English church find itself in dispute with the English king?" began Pope Paschal.

"The king demands that I give in to his arbitrary demands in the name of justice," answered Anselm. "But his demands are against the will of God. I ask you not to send me back to England until I can put the will of God before the will of men."

"Why does the king persist in this conversation?" asked the pope.

Warelwast cleared his throat. "It is within the king's rights to choose his own bishops. Monarchs before Henry have done so without provoking Rome's anger. It is now an expectation of his subjects."

The pope looked at Anselm, but he remained quiet.

"Have you nothing more to say, archbishop?"

Anselm lowered his head. "I have already described the situation to you. I came here to seek direction, not to give it. I dare not presume to know more than the council of Rome."

"Do you mean that Henry presumes to know more than Rome?"

Warelwast leaned forward. "Henry is not setting himself against the church. But the king's wishes—the wishes of a great man—should not be simply overlooked." The pope did not reply, so he continued. "A king is the ruler of his land. His rule will never be effective if his power is stripped from him. Not even to save his kingdom can King Henry give up his established right to invest bishops."

The pope drew in a sharp breath. "Nor, to save his own head, will this pope give in to any king's demands! The council ruled on this issue several years ago. If Henry invests bishops without the approval of the church, he and those he invests will be excommunicated."

The council murmured. Warelwast glanced at them, the corners of his mouth twitching.

"We have heard your arguments," said the pope. "Return to your king. The council will inform you of our final word by letter."

"Paschal is not a politician," Anselm told Eadmer as they prepared to leave. "But there are quite a few of them on that council. They don't want a fight with Henry."

They spent Christmas in Lyons, rather than travel all the way back to England. Warelwast met them there. "I bring a message from the king."

"That can't be good," Eadmer mumbled under his breath.

The lawyer ignored him. "Before I left England, the king made it clear that you are only welcome to return if you pay homage and consecrate his bishops."

"We have not yet heard the council's decision! Until then, he can make no demands."

Warelwast shrugged. "If you refuse, he will seize your lands and revenues."

"Then I will not be returning to England," replied the archbishop, shaking his head. "Leave me."

As soon as Warelwast departed, Anselm told Eadmer to get his pen. "Take down the following letter: *To his revered Lord, Henry, King of the English, from Anselm, Archbishop of Canterbury, with faithful service and prayers.*" He paused, searching for the right words, and then began again. "*William of Warelwast will report to you on our meetings in Rome. I wish that I could assume the same relationship with you that my predecessor had with your father. But I cannot do homage, nor hold communion with those who have received investiture at your hands. I pray that you will allow me to return to England on these terms, with your peace and with the authority that belongs to my office. If this does not please you, I suppose that the loss of souls that may result in my absence will not be held to my account.*"

He hesitated again.

"Is that all, master?" asked Eadmer.

"Yes. No—wait. Close it this way: *May God Almighty so reign in your heart that you may reign forever in his grace."*

Anselm moved to the door, and then turned back. "Send the original to the king, of course. But make a copy and send that to my friend Gundulf, Bishop of Rochester. I don't trust that Warelwast. If he tries anything funny with the letter, Gundulf can verify that it came from me."

There was no reply from Henry. Anselm wrote to him three times, demanding that he return the property. Matilda wrote to say that the king had received the letters, but he would not respond. She promised Anselm that she was pleading with her husband to relent.

Two years passed. An unexpected visitor arrived in Lyons in early summer. "One of the queen's ladies requests an audience with you, master," Eadmer announced to Anselm, who was busy writing in his study.

"Who is she?"

"Adele, Countess of Blois."

Anselm looked up from his manuscript with eyebrows raised. "The king's sister?"

"Yes, master."

He nodded and rose to his feet as she entered.

"Thank you for seeing me, archbishop," said the countess.

He took her gloved hand and led her to a couch. She folded back the lace mantle that covered her head, revealing wisps of graying hair at her temples. Her face was troubled.

"To what do I owe the honor of your visit?" he asked.

"The queen was thrilled to receive the book of prayers you composed. She wants you to know that she now uses them in her own devotions."

"I'm pleased to hear it."

Her smile faded. "When I told Matilda I would be traveling though Lyons, she asked me to see you. She begs you to return to England."

"I have received her letters," he said, frowning, "and I've already notified her of my decision."

"Won't you reconsider?"

"I cannot. If I return, I would be forced to fellowship with the corrupt clergy who support Henry."

"But how long can this standoff with the king continue? Isn't there some way you can end it?"

"I can excommunicate Henry myself if he does not restore my property."

"Excommunicate! Henry is preparing to take Normandy from his brother Robert. If he is cast out of the church now, the nobles will withdraw their support. It would be a disaster for him!"

"He has given me no other recourse!"

"Please talk to him, archbishop. If I can convince Henry to listen, will you agree to meet with him?"

He hesitated. "I do not think he will agree."

"Leave that to me." She kissed his hand and, collecting her skirts, left as quickly as she could with the dignity of a countess.

A month later, a message arrived from Normandy. The king had agreed to meet with the archbishop on the battlefront. Anselm set out with Eadmer at his side.

Henry's knights had established their camp on an estate near the border town of Laigle. The grassy slopes were dotted with canvas tents, each one proudly flying Henry's banner. Two horsemen escorted the archbishop's carriage past the smoky cooking fires and the makeshift corrals, where clouds of buzzing flies annoyed the horses. A large tent loomed at the center of the camp.

Anselm stepped down from his coach with difficulty, feeling in his knees the aches of age and travel. His forehead was damp with perspiration under the July sun. He mopped it absently with his sleeve.

"It is good to see you well, archbishop."

Henry stood at the entrance, where the tent's flaps had been tied open. He had left behind his colorful brocade and lace, and was dressed instead like one of his knights in a tunic of fine chain mail and leather leggings. Only the crown over his skullcap declared his royal rank.

Anselm nodded in a stiff bow. "You are kind to be concerned about my well being."

"I'll do more than that and offer you some refreshment. Come inside."

The ground inside the tent was covered by a large rug, with two chairs and a table at the center. Eadmer helped Anselm into a chair and then withdrew to a shadowy corner. Henry dropped into the remaining chair and poured two drinks from a jug.

"I regret that I don't have much time to talk," the king began. "As you can see, we are preparing for battle. Normandy and England will soon be reunited."

"At the expense of your brother's rule," replied Anselm.

Henry's dark eyes flashed. "I did not ask you here to bless my invasion. The queen and her ladies have been most insistent that I try again to reach a common ground with you."

"The ground in question is my estate, which you have wrongly confiscated."

"Any noble who neglects to pay me tribute will find himself in the same position."

"I am not *any* noble. I am your spiritual father, and it is my duty to be concerned about the condition of your heart."

"You find my heart so evil that you threaten to excommunicate me?"

"You have forced my hand."

"Excommunication is the severest punishment the church can pronounce. Is that not for the pope to decide?"

"My property is my authority. It is not an issue for Rome."

Henry glared at him across the table, but Anselm did not flinch.

"You are the strictest man of principle I know," the king said finally. "I cannot afford to lose my support now. You win, archbishop. If you promise not to put me out of the church, I will return your lands."

"You are a gracious man, sire."

Henry scowled and rose from his seat.

"We still have other unfinished business," Anselm said.

"Those issues are in the hands of the pope, and I believe he sees my point of view."

"The council has not yet ruled. It isn't wise to make assumptions."

"I can spare no time to discuss this further. I have a war to win!" He stalked away, but turned back at the entrance. "Give my greetings to the queen and her ladies when you pass through Salisbury." And then he was gone.

The archbishop and his assistant left the camp immediately.

"I assume we will be returning to England now that your lands have been restored?" Eadmer asked as they reached the main road outside of Laigle.

Anselm shook his head. "I can't go back until the council clarifies their position on homage and investiture. Until they do, I risk my soul by praying and serving with clergy who have not been ordained properly."

Eadmer located a house to rent in Normandy. Anselm was determined to wait out the council. Nearly a year passed before a sealed message arrived from Rome.

"What does it say?" Anselm asked.

Eadmer opened the letter and scanned it. "A compromise has been reached," he said, the corners of his mouth twitching in distaste. "In the interests of church unity, Henry will be allowed to demand homage from the bishops. But he is not allowed to invest clergy, or he will face excommunication."

Anselm sank into his chair. "I had a feeling the council would allow politics to get in the way."

"The letter suggests that you interpreted the earlier decision of the council too strictly."

"I did no such thing!"

Eadmer said nothing.

The archbishop scratched his bald spot. "But Rome has declared the church's position, and I am bound to obey."

"It is a difficult ruling to accept, master."

"It is. But in a way, I suppose it is good news. Henry will accept the compromise, so we will no longer be at odds."

"We will return to Canterbury?"

He nodded. "We will return to Canterbury."

Eadmer folded away the letter. "The queen will be pleased."

"Yes, and I can finally perform the duties of archbishop in peace, like my master Lanfranc did before me." He rose. "Come, we have work to do."

Within a week, they set out for England again. This time, their stay would be permanent.

Anselm returned to England in 1106, but Henry was away for a year, invading Normandy. He captured Duke Robert, imprisoning him in Cardiff Castle, where the duke remained until his death thirty years later.

After Henry returned to England, he and Anselm agreed to a full reconciliation. Anselm spent the last year and a half of his life in peaceful fulfillment of his duties, for the first time since he had taken the office. He died in 1109. Henry waited five years before choosing a successor, in the meantime keeping the revenues of the estate for himself.

After his master's death, Eadmer published his Life of Anselm. *The book is now our most valuable source of details about the archbishop's career.*

What were the Crusades?

CHRISTIANITY SPREAD RAPIDLY during the Middle Ages. So did an opposing religion called *Islam* (see the feature, "What is Islam?," page 63). Christianity and Islam became popular for many reasons. Sometimes people accepted one of these religions because they truly believed in its teachings. Other times they accepted a particular religion because their homeland was conquered by rulers who were either Christian or Muslim.

By the year 1000, Muslims controlled most of the area in the Middle East known as the *Holy Land*. At first, Muslim rulers allowed Christians to go on *pilgrimages*, or devotional visits, to the city of Jerusalem. The *pilgrims* wanted to see where Jesus had taught and climb the hill where he had died. Muslim rulers allowed the Christian pilgrims to visit these sites in peace, as long as they paid taxes. But as political differences grew between Muslim and Christian rulers, the Muslims began to limit the pilgrims' visits to the Holy Land.

Christians believed that the Holy Land should be under their rule, since they were followers of Jesus. But Muslims and Christians traced their ancestors back to the biblical figure Abraham, so both believed they had rights to the land. Christian and Muslim rulers began to clash.

Since 1054, the Christian church had been divided between the east (Constantinople) and the west (Rome). (See the feature, "A Divided Church: The Great Schism of 1054.") After a series of clashes between the eastern church and their Muslim neighbors, Christians in the east asked the western church to join them in a *Crusade* to fight the Muslims.

The western church hoped that by working with their eastern brothers against a common threat, they would heal the division between the two sides of the church. So Pope Urban II (1042-1099) and a preacher named Peter the Hermit (1050-1115) called the people to war in 1096.

Thousands of men, women, and children volunteered to join the Crusade. Some did it because they believed Jerusalem belonged to Christians. Their battle cry became, "God wills it!" Others did it because the pope told them God would forgive all of their sins if they helped defeat the Muslims. And some were simply ambitious men seeking fame, power, and riches.

The *Crusaders* captured Jerusalem. The church soon established a military order called the *Knights Templar*. They took vows like monks, and dedicated their swords to protecting pilgrims and defending the Holy Land. The *Knights Hospitallers* were based in a hospital in Jerusalem, and vowed to care for the sick.

They maintained control of the city for nearly a century. But as they fought among themselves, they gradually lost their power. A key defense city, Edessa, fell to the Muslims in 1144.

So a Second Crusade was called, and again the people were stirred to action by a preacher. An abbot named Bernard of

Clairvaux was one of many Christians who were convinced that God wanted the church to regain the Holy Land. His sermons inspired thousands of Crusaders.

There were Christians who opposed the Crusades. Anselm, Archbishop of Canterbury, objected to war. He argued that Christians should reason with Muslims, and convert them to Christianity instead of force them out of the Holy Land.

The Crusaders became even more power hungry. Like before, they fought against each other, and the Second Crusade was a complete failure. Thousands died before they ever reached Jerusalem.

But the Crusades continued. In 1189, a Third Crusade was led by Holy Roman Emperor Frederick Barbarossa (1123-1190), King Philip Augustus (1165-1223) of France, and King Richard "The Lion-Hearted" (1157-1199) of England. It was more successful than the previous attempt.

In 1202, the Fourth Crusade was called by Pope Innocent III (1160-1216), but instead of fighting against the Muslims, Crusaders from the west plundered the city of Constantinople. The eastern empire became weak, and was eventually conquered by Muslims in 1453.

Four more Crusades followed between the years of 1217 and 1270.

In the end, Jerusalem remained under Muslim control. The eastern and western churches became more divided than before. And the gospel of Christ had been polluted by violence. The Crusades became a sad and horrifying period of the history of the Christian church.

Bernard of Clairvaux: Did you lead us here to die?

NOVEMBER 28, 1144. EDESSA, NOW URFA IN MODERN-DAY TURKEY.

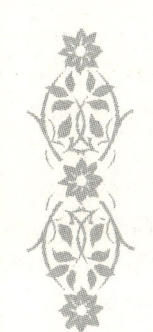

VULTURES CIRCLED OMINOUSLY over Edessa. Like a jewel in a setting of fine gold, the city was an oasis in the shimmering sands of Mesopotamia. Rumored to be the birthplace of Abraham, the father of many nations, it was an outpost along the route to Jerusalem.

After the success of the First Crusade, European knights controlled much of the Holy Land in the name of the church. But Muslim rulers began to regain the advantage, capturing one city at a time. A Muslim army intent on conquering the Holy Land would have to first capture Edessa.

That was just what Zengi intended to do.

The Turkish general halted his horse on a ridge above the city and surveyed what would soon be his prize. Behind him, a swarm of troops stretched across the horizon, their mail hauberks layered under tunics of rich blue, yellow, and green. Each bore his weapon of choice: a bow, a light spear, or the cruel curved blade of a scimitar.

"Edessa is weak," the general observed, stroking his black beard.

"There are few men on the fortifications."

His lieutenant, a young man in a turban with a scimitar strapped to his back, shaded his eyes and peered across the sand at the sun-bleached walls. "Reports say many of the Christian knights are away. Only a handful remain in the city."

"They know we are here."

"Even if they had no scouts, the vultures would tell them that." He squinted up at the huge birds hovering in the hot sky. "But it matters not. They are no match for our numbers or speed."

Zengi jerked his head toward the city. "Go."

He watched as his lieutenant crossed the rippled dunes, riding to within a few paces of the city gates. Behind his horse streamed a green banner bearing a crescent moon and a single star. He waited, alone, the sands shifting under his stallion's hooves.

The gates were raised just high enough to release a mounted Crusader with a pointed shield, a bright red cross painted boldly across the center. The sun glinted off his helmet as he met the Turk, his horse nose-to-nose with the other stallion.

The exchange took only moments. It was just a formality, and both sides knew the results before the messengers parted, riding back to their respective armies.

"The infidels will not surrender," said the Turkish lieutenant, tearing up the ridge back to his general.

Zengi sighed and mopped the sweat from his forehead. "I expected as much. It is a shame to spill so much blood for a city."

"They will gladly spill ours to defend it!"

"They will have to. We will take this city no matter the cost."

"Yes, general."

"Send the catapults in. The archers will follow."

"Yes, general." The lieutenant shouted the signal to his captains.

General Zengi swung around on his muscular horse and thrust his scimitar over his head. "Praise be to God! We will take what is rightfully ours!"

The army cheered and surged forward.

Atop the city walls, the knights rallied their defenses. "Get foot soldiers to the gates and archers to the towers!"

Clouds of dust choked the streets as the residents fled for cover.

"You!" yelled a knight, snatching one of the men by his arm. "Pick up a sword and defend your city!"

"I'm not a knight!" stammered the man, flailing his empty hands to show he had no weapon. "I'm just a merchant. I buy and sell and bargain. I'm not a fighter!"

"What good is your business if you are dead?" roared the knight, forcing an axe into the man's hands and shoving him toward the wall. "You've just been knighted. Now fight!"

The bewildered merchant stumbled toward the walls, where a remnant of Crusaders waited, swords drawn, for the Turkish army.

"We must hold them off until Count Joscelin returns," shouted one knight to his brother-at-arms.

"Joscelin is cut off now. He couldn't help us even if we got a message to him."

They steadied themselves as the first volley from the catapults struck the tower.

"Look! Those are Byzantine catapults!"

"They must have captured them in a previous battle."

A shower of burning arrows rained down, sending a cloud of smoke drifting across the walls.

"Joscelin is a fool for leaving this city undefended! What good is it to have towers and walls if there are no knights to guard them?"

"Listen to me, all of you!" cried their leader. "Each of us has vowed to protect these pilgrims. With God's grace, we'll fight as a thousand men!"

They raised their swords as one and shouted, "Glory to the God of Heaven!"

And so the siege began. By the following March, the whole world knew the fate of Edessa. The news reached even the quietest chambers of the abbey of Clairvaux in France.

"Pope Eugene wants me to do what?"

The question echoed through the dim wine cellar below the ground floor of the sprawling abbey. A thin man with a fringe of gray hair stared at his younger companion in disbelief.

The young man gave his leader a reassuring smile. "I'm sure he will give you time to think about his request, abbot."

"It doesn't sound like he's giving me a choice at all!" declared Abbot Bernard. "First King Louis pesters me to help him raise an army of Crusaders—you know I refused—and now the pope wants me to do the same."

"Pope Eugene knows how powerful your preaching is. People will join the Crusade if you convince them it is God's will."

Abbot Bernard shook his head and brushed cobwebs from a wooden cask he was inspecting. "The church's focus should be private worship and teaching Scripture to our brothers here, Geoffrey, not converting Muslims in other kingdoms."

"The pope disagrees with you."

"The pope was once my pupil in this very abbey. He knows I don't like to travel. Clairvaux is my whole life."

"With respect, abbot, the church is much bigger than Clairvaux. Eugene is pope now, and he needs your help."

Bernard laughed suddenly and began to pace in front of the casks. The rows of dusty cylinders next to him were barely visible in the shadows. "He has already promised eternal life to those who join the cause!" he said, throwing up his hands. "If that's not enough to motivate people, there are also titles and lands to win and adventures to be had. Do they really need more reasons?"

Geoffrey stepped into the abbot's path. "Bernard, you are my friend, so I will speak candidly." He paused. "Edessa has fallen to the Muslims. Eugene, your former student and now your spiritual head, has called a Second Crusade to regain the land. He is asking you to rouse the people to battle."

Bernard looked away.

"Your father was a brave knight of Châtillon who fought in the First Crusade," Geoffrey reminded him. "If you did not believe in the cause, why did you write the rule for the Order of the Knights Templar?"

Bernard stepped around his assistant and headed toward the stairs.

"There is no one better fit to stir the people to action!" Geoffrey called after him.

The abbot disappeared up the staircase, leaving Geoffrey alone in the musty cellar.

All night the candles flickered in Bernard's cell as he paced, hands behind his back. Spread out on his desk was a large, single page. The text was copied in the beautiful calligraphy developed in the monasteries, and signed with the pope's seal.

To the illustrious King Louis of France, and to his princes, and to all Christians who are eager to help their brothers and to fight for the dignity of the church, I offer my blessing.

The sons of the holy church gave their blood to free from the pagans that city where our Savior suffered for us. By God's grace we have held that city. But now another city, Edessa, has fallen. The archbishop and his clergy and many other Christians have been slain by the pagans. It is time to prove that the nobility and bravery of your fathers has been passed on to the sons! Defend your captive brothers that the dignity of Christ's name will spread throughout the world.

All who set out on this sacred journey and who confess their sins with a humble heart shall receive the fruit of eternal life.

Bernard broke off pacing and read the document a second time, stared at the wall, read it again. He dropped to his knees in prayer, and after a while started pacing again. The pattern continued all night.

An early-rising rooster was just beginning to crow when Bernard woke Geoffrey with a shake.

"What is it, abbot?"

"Get up and send a message."

"Now?"

"I don't do anything halfway. If I'm going to preach the Crusade, I'm going to do it right. Tell King Louis I will meet him in Vézelay on Palm Sunday."

Geoffrey rubbed his eyes and pulled his scratchy cowl over his head. He would have just enough time to dispatch a messenger before morning prayers began.

The week before Easter was clear and cool. Arriving in Vézelay at dusk, Bernard and Geoffrey went straight to the Basilica of Saint Mary Magdalene and gratefully accepted the stewed rabbit offered by the hospitable bishop. But in the morning, they were directed not to the sanctuary but to a field just outside the city.

"Your reputation has drawn a huge crowd," explained the bishop. "The people will not fit inside the church, so the king built a platform outside. You will preach from there."

The narrow streets were crowded with people jostling to get out into the country. It was Sunday, and they had scrubbed their hands and faces and left their tools at home. But tucked into their ragged cloaks were loaves of black bread and skins of water.

"They're expecting a long sermon today," said Bernard, adjusting his crimson robes as they followed the bishop through the crowd.

Geoffrey laughed. "Your reputation precedes you!"

The road curved away from the city, and a wooden platform in the clearing came suddenly into view. Supported by heavy pillars, it held a row of sturdy benches behind a slightly raised podium. A simple staircase, flanked by Louis' guards, rose from the ground. It was still early in the season, and the grasses were only ankle-high.

The bishop nodded at Bernard. "Go on up. The king and queen will be joining you."

Geoffrey followed Bernard up the narrow wooden stairs, dragging a bulging sack behind him. From the top of the platform, they looked down on a sea of faces noisily awaiting the king's arrival. Stretching across the greening fields and over the pointed rooftops beyond, the sky was blue and cloudless. Bernard wondered if the weather might turn warmer by the end of the day. A shout arose from below the platform, and the abbot and his assistant made way for the king as he reached the top of the stairs.

"Abbot Bernard! What a pleasure to finally see you in Vézelay." Louis bowed low before his guests in a ceremonial gesture. A velvet cap covered his hair, worn long and curled under in a smooth roll below his ears.

He turned aside and reached down to help the queen up the last rung. She took his hand, drawing up her skirts behind her with her other hand. She, too, wore velvet, a long embroidered cape of sapphire blue, fastened to the neckline of her bodice with jewels. She flashed a smile at Bernard and allowed Louis to arrange her skirts as she took her place on the bench.

A herald blew a short blast on his horn and cried, "King Louis, illustrious sovereign of France, and Queen Eleanor of Aquitaine!"

The crowd broke into loud cheers.

Louis stood and acknowledged the people, but insisted that Bernard take the podium. "Bernard, of the abbey of Clairvaux, will address us on this first day of Holy Week."

A hush fell over the field as Bernard stepped into the podium.

"Pope Eugene, the Holy Father, has sent me here to bless our king and his people." He half-turned to Louis and nodded.

Beaming, Louis nodded back.

Geoffrey stepped forward with the pope's letter, holding it as Bernard read aloud the call for the people to join the crusade. Whispers rippled through the crowd, but their eyes remained fixed on the abbot's face.

Geoffrey stepped back.

"To join this mission," declared Bernard, "is an act of love for God. We know we must obey God, we must fear God, we must worship God. But why must we love God?" He leaned over the wooden railing and gazed down at the people. "Because God is love! God is his own reason for loving him. Only in loving God can we find happiness. The perfect, powerful creator of the world calls you to love him. He calls you to serve his church with your lives!"

From the folds of his crimson mantle, Bernard pulled a small bundle. It was heavy for its size, and he unwrapped it carefully. The crowd strained to see what he held in his hands.

He suddenly raised the object high over his head. The sunlight glinted off its smooth surface so that it seemed almost to glow.

"This cross," shouted Bernard, "is a gift from Pope Eugene. He presents it now to our excellent king with the commission to restore the dignity of the church."

Louis kneeled on the platform. Bernard draped the chain around the king's neck, centering the golden cross on his brocade vest.

His eyes sparkling, Louis stood and held the cross off his chest for the crowd to see. They shouted their happy approval.

Bernard raised his hands to quiet the people as Louis returned to his seat beside the queen.

"Citizens of the kingdom of God," he cried, "now is the acceptable time! Today is the day of salvation! You have heard of the desolation of Edessa. On account of our sins, the enemies of the cross of Christ have raised their mouths in blasphemy and devastated the Holy Land, the Land of Promise, with fire and sword. We must repent!"

The field was silent with shame.

"Unless they are opposed, these enemies will dare to burst into the city of the Living God and destroy the remaining precious memorials of our redemption," he continued boldly. "You gallant knights, what will you do? Onward, Christian soldiers! Reconcile the Holy Land to God with your swords."

"God wills it!" the people shouted.

"As in the days when Peter the Hermit led us to victory in Jerusalem, we must gather our best to lead us to victory under the banner of the cross!"

A thunderous cry went up from the crowd. "Give us the cross! Give us the cross!"

Louis leaned over and whispered into the queen's ear. "Eugene was right. If anyone can stir the people to battle, it is this abbot."

Bernard was shouting now, his voice ringing out over the clamor. "The cross was a symbol of the Great Crusade. Under this cross, my father and other sons of France helped restore the land of Christ once before. Under this cross we will do so again!"

Geoffrey tore open the sack at his feet and held up a cross cut from scarlet wool.

"Who will come receive the cross?" demanded Bernard.

The first in line to receive a cross was Queen Eleanor. She knelt before him, bowing her fair, shining head as he touched it in blessing. She clutched the sacred symbol to herself as Geoffrey handed it to her.

Behind her waited the queen's brother and uncle, both accepting their crosses with reverence.

Bernard climbed down the stairs with Geoffrey dragging the sack behind him. The crowd pressed forward. Thousands of hands reached out to snatch up the crosses.

"They're gone, abbot!" Geoffrey shouted. "The bag is empty."

Bernard pulled off his red mantle and began to tear it into strips. He handed out the pieces until there were no more.

"You are the man Eugene said you were," bowed Louis. "I will inform him of your success today and prepare for you to preach throughout France." He turned before Bernard had a chance to respond, and allowed his guards to sweep him toward his carriage.

Bernard preached several more times that week. Immediately after Easter, he and Geoffrey began to make their way from town to town, stirring the people of France to join the Crusade. At each stop, farmers, blacksmiths, merchants, and noblemen gathered supplies and prepared to journey to the Holy Land.

"Hermann, bishop of Constance, asks you to take your preaching to Germany," Geoffrey informed him one day as he sorted through Bernard's letters. "The emperor grants his permission, although he has not yet decided if he will support the cause."

"I don't know. We've been away from Clairvaux for months," replied Bernard. "I have responsibilities there."

"The Crusade cannot succeed without Germany."

"It is true." Bernard frowned and ran a hand over his smooth head. "Let Hermann know we will set out at once. I intend to be back at Clairvaux by the end of the year."

They arrived in Frankfurt in December. Bishop Hermann was all smiles as he hurried out to greet them.

"Welcome to Germany, good Bernard!"

"Thank you. I hope you will not be offended that my time is limited. I hope to return to France shortly."

Hermann's fleshly face fell. "But it is Advent! I was hoping you would stay with me in Constance through the holy season. Besides, Conrad is being crowned Emperor of the Holy Roman Empire on Christmas Day, in the tradition of Charlemagne. You must not miss the celebration!"

Geoffrey gave his abbot a meaningful look. "It is an historic occasion, abbot. And there are many people here who have not heard your message. Perhaps you will consider his offer?"

"Perhaps."

"Wonderful!" said Hermann, smiling again. "Many of us are eager to defend the name of Christ. I wish that I were younger so I could join the fight myself! We have heard so much about your preaching. It is said that you are very convincing."

Geoffrey broke in. "The abbot speaks, and the number of Crusaders multiplies. In the villages of France, you are hard pressed to find one man for every seven women. They're all away preparing for battle."

Hermann clapped his hands. "Ah! That is proof that God is blessing the Crusade! And now you must convince the Germans."

"I've heard that many of the princes are against it."

"Yes, but Conrad has not yet made up his mind. You may succeed where I and others have failed."

They spent the weeks of Advent preaching through Germany, arriving at Spier by boat on Christmas Eve. The city was full of bishops and princes invited for the coronation. As soon as Conrad heard Bernard was in town, he offered him a seat among the honored guests.

The coronation was a solemn ceremony, followed by music and colorful pageantry. But all eyes were on the new emperor and the famous preacher who had come to spur him to battle.

On the day after Christmas, Bernard appeared at Conrad's palace unannounced.

"Welcome, good Bernard!" said the emperor in surprise. He pointed to his companions. "My nephew, Frederick, and General Luder, one of my advisors."

Bernard nodded in turn at the red-bearded noble with sharp

eyes, and at the stocky general, who nervously fingered his drooping mustache.

"I'm surprised you are not preparing for the Feast of Saint John tomorrow," said Conrad. His smile was warm, but his fingers rapped impatiently on the table at his side.

"I will finish my sermon tonight. But now, may I have a word with you in private, your excellency?"

Frederick and Luder began to speak, but the emperor raised a forbidding hand.

"Leave us."

They departed immediately.

Conrad crossed his arms over his broad chest and got to his feet. "You are here to convince me to join the Crusade?"

"You are not convinced by the pope's letter?"

"No."

Bernard bent at the waist in a stiff bow. "It is not my place to question the king's majesty. But I must urge him to think of his soul while the pope seeks leaders for a holy war."

"I am no Moses or Joshua leading God's people out of Egypt."

"You are far greater!" insisted Bernard. "You are the leader of the Holy Roman Empire!"

Conrad turned to face him directly, towering over the slight abbot. "What assurance do I have that we will win?"

"You have the blessing of the church and the evidence that God is moving thousands to join this mission."

The emperor stared at his feet thoughtfully. "I will speak to my counselors," he said finally. "You will know my decision tomorrow."

Bernard thanked him and left.

As soon as he was gone, Frederick and Luder rushed in.

"Did you tell the abbot you would join the Crusade, uncle?" Frederick questioned.

Conrad frowned at him. "Is none of my business secret?"

"Bernard's cause is no secret. Consider what he has to say, I beg you. The Crusade would be a remarkable adventure."

"Are you hoping your uncle will die in battle so you can inherit the throne?"

"Of course not! But Germany's knights can secure a glorious victory for the church."

Luder stepped in front of Frederick. "Ignore your nephew and the abbot. They are not concerned for your empire. The bishop of Rome wants this battle, not the Germans."

"Do you speak for all of Germany?"

"I speak for many of her princes, as well as many of her bishops. Not all Christians believe in these crusades, your excellency. Many believe you should convert men through argument, changing their hearts, rather than forcing them to believe with a sword."

"Tell that to the Muslims who slaughtered our brothers!" objected Conrad.

"Your excellency——."

"That's enough," insisted Conrad, "from both of you. I promised Bernard an answer tomorrow and I need time to think." He swept out of the room and left them glaring at each other.

The Feast of Saint John drew crowds of people to the cathedral in Frankfurt. Bernard was pleased to see the emperor present with many of his knights. *The Lord has brought them here for a reason*, he thought.

He fixed his eyes on Conrad and began to preach. "It is a high calling to obey God. But it is a calling with assured blessing. Those who are not willing to follow Christ here on earth, will not follow him in heaven. The last judgment shall remove them from his presence, and hell will await them!"

The congregation glanced at the emperor and shifted in their seats.

"Will you stand before his throne in heaven and ask what

more he wanted you to do?" continued Bernard. "Do you want God to answer that you should have used what he gave you for his purposes? Emperor, God has granted you health, power, and greatness of character. Will you keep it for yourself or use it to do his will?"

He stopped, unsure how the emperor would respond, but certain he had made his point.

Conrad's eyes shone as he approached the altar where Bernard stood. "Thank you, abbot. I see that my crown is a divine gift, and I shall not be found ungrateful. I am ready to obey God and devote myself to recapturing his holy city."

The people came to their feet, shouting, "God wills it!"

Bernard snatched up the golden cross on top of the altar, kissed it, and presented it to Conrad.

"You are God's Moses, not me," the emperor whispered as he took the statue. "You have convinced me to join your cause."

"It is not my cause," said Bernard. "It is the pope's cause, the church's cause. With divine blessing, you cannot fail."

Conrad turned to face the people, raising the cross high over his head. "God wills it!" he cried.

"God wills it!" they shouted back.

It took months for the armies to assemble. As Conrad gathered his forces in Germany, Bernard and Geoffrey returned to France, where Louis' soldiers were preparing to depart. The pope himself came to Paris on Easter to bless the king and his troops.

It was a glorious morning when the Crusaders set off toward the Holy Land, with Louis in his saddle at the lead. They were to meet up with Conrad on the way, and pick up troops from England, Italy, and Hungary. Exhausted, homesick, and convinced he had done all he could, Bernard gratefully returned to his quiet monastery.

The abbot was sitting on the bare floorboards in his room at

Clairvaux when Geoffrey appeared, grim-faced, at his door.

"I beg your pardon, abbot. I would never disturb your prayers, but..."

"What is it?"

"A rider has arrived with news from the Holy Land. The Crusaders are returning."

Bernard peered at his assistant with alarm. "But it has not even been a year! A quick victory?"

"You must hear it for yourself."

He followed Geoffrey through the vaulted arches and out to the courtyard. A light snow was falling. The oversized flakes swirled in the shifting air currents, melting as they came to rest on the cobblestones. Bernard shivered in his thin robe and drew his hands up into his sleeves.

"Damascus is lost to the Muslims." The knight sagged in his saddle, the cross on his chest tattered and stained.

The abbot stared at him.

"What happened?" asked Geoffrey.

"Louis and Conrad were out for themselves. They stopped to fight their own battles on the way. Many were lost before they even reached the Holy Land! The Emperor of Constantinople promised many ships, but sent only a few. By the time Louis and Conrad agreed to take Damascus, Muslim defenses were in place. It was a miserable failure!"

"But God willed it!" cried Geoffrey.

The knight gave a short, bitter laugh. "You would not say so if you had been there."

"Where are Louis and Conrad?" Bernard's voice was barely audible.

"On their way home, where they will be humiliated." The knight glared at Bernard and tossed a package at Geoffrey's feet. "The Crusaders who know how to write have sent you some love letters."

With that, he turned his horse and sped off toward the road.

Bernard stared up the gray sky, letting the icy flakes drift into his cowl and prick his neck like tiny needles.

"Come on, abbot. Let's go inside."

Geoffrey picked up the package and turned back toward the door, but Bernard remained where he stood, shivering, gazing up at the snow.

"Read them," he said.

"What?"

"The letters. Read them."

Geoffrey plucked at the abbot's thin sleeve. "Let's go warm up in the kitchen and then we'll read them."

Bernard turned steely eyes on him. "Now."

He drew out a stack of pages, letting the sack drop to the wet pavement. His eyes flickered over the first one. Frowning, he began to shuffle it to the bottom, but Bernard reached out and snatched it.

Did you lead us here to die? The characters were written in a large, angry hand. *You promised us victory, but now we are mocked by the enemy more than we were before!* The page slipped out of his trembling fingers.

Geoffrey scooped it up. Little blotches of ink began to run on the paper. He put it back on the stack and tucked it all into his belt.

Bernard's voice was flat. "When Moses led the Israelites out of Egypt, he promised them a better land. He spoke what the Lord commanded him to speak."

"As did you, Bernard. The Crusade was not your idea. You refused the king twice and only took up the cause when the pope himself ordered you to preach."

"Which means it was God's will!" the abbot cried.

Geoffrey was silent.

The flakes were falling faster now, and beginning to stick to the cobblestones. Already the shrubs were covered in a white layer.

"The Israelites wandered in the wilderness for forty years blaming Moses and blaming God," said Bernard. "Generations missed out on God's promises."

"Israel suffered because of their sins. So have the Crusaders, who went to battle for personal gain. They secretly longed to return to captivity rather than enter the promised land."

"And now the name of Christ is tarnished, like the sword of that knight who would have spat on me if he was not a decent man!" He passed a cold hand over his eyes. "If someone must be blamed, I would rather it be me than God. I will gladly be humiliated to shield God's glory from attack."

"Please come inside now, abbot. The cold air is not good for your health."

Bernard looked away. "Leave me," he said quietly.

Geoffrey went inside then, and the powerful abbot stood alone in the courtyard, tears mingling with the snowflakes on his upturned face.

Bernard devoted himself to founding dozens of abbeys throughout France, and writing books which inspired generations of Christians, including a famous theologian named John Calvin. The failure of the Second Crusade haunted him for the rest of his life, but the church did not learn from the experience. Six more crusades would be attempted in the following centuries.

Conrad's nephew, Frederick (nicknamed Barbarossa *or "red beard"), became Holy Roman Emperor. He drowned crossing a river while leading the Third Crusade.*

Francis: A Knight in Monk's Clothing

1205. ASSISI, IN CENTRAL ITALY.

THE SUN HAD set an hour ago, and the dark piazza was deserted except for a young man in an odd patchwork cloak. Like all towns, the streets of Assisi could be dangerous at night, but he walked confidently across the familiar square. Over his left shoulder towered the cathedral. Behind it, tall houses of nobles climbed the mountainside. To his right, across the piazza, began the jumble of narrow wooden houses rented by the working class.

The sounds of laughter and a fiddle drew him to a tavern at the far corner of the piazza. A dim patch of light fell across the step as he flung open the door.

"I hear songs of Charlemagne and the Knights of the Round Table!" he shouted.

Two young men jumped up from their table.

"Francis has returned!" cried Thomas.

"And he is over-dressed even for knight," laughed Angelo.

Francis threw a bag of money to the tavern keeper. "This should cover my friends and I for the night," he said. "We have a lot of catching up to do!"

Thomas and Angelo slapped him on the back and drew him to their table. "Tell us what happened out there, Francis."

"The stinking Perugians stripped me of my armor and weapons! They would have killed me if they had known I was just a squire. Mother said it was my vanity that saved me since I had insisted on dressing like a knight." He shook his head. "It cost my father a load of his best silk to replace that exquisite sword."

"It cost him a lot more than that to pay the ransom for you and bring you home from that dungeon!"

"He only paid it because he was ashamed I had been captured."

Thomas frowned suddenly. "Be thankful that you were spared, Francis. Many of Assisi's sons died in the Battle of Collestrada."

Francis grew quiet. "I know that better than you. I saw the broken bodies of our friends on that battlefield as the Perugians dragged me off."

His companions looked away.

"Assisi wasn't ready for that fight," said Angelo.

"We still aren't. And I'm tired of this civil war," said Francis. "I've pledged my new sword to Count Gentile as his squire. We're joining Walter de Brienne's campaign in Apulia against the Germans."

Thomas stared at him. "Surely your father objects to you going off to battle again!"

"He can't tell me what to do! I'm a grown man now, and I'm going to make my own fortune as a knight."

"Peter Bernadone is a shrewd businessman. He's not going to keep supporting you if you don't help him with his cloth business. I doubt even the count is as wealthy as your father."

Francis shrugged. "Lady Chivalry cannot be so easily dismissed. To fight noble battles, to meet beautiful women, to inspire troubadours to sing of my exploits! That is what I was born to do, like Charlemagne and Walter de Brienne."

Francis waved the tavern keeper to their table. "Another round, my man. To Walter and the life of chivalry!"

"To Walter!" they shouted.

Thomas drained his mug and stood. "In honor of his return, I declare 'Sir' Francis the Lord of the Revels!"

"Only someone with his wardrobe could have such a title!" declared Angelo with a wink. "Where did that ridiculous cloak come from anyway?"

"I made it."

"Why did you use a dozen different fabrics?"

"Because I can."

Angelo burst into laughter. "What songs you shall inspire!" He threw his head back and bowed his fiddle. "These are the tales of Sir Francis," he crooned, "who slayed the silk and captured the velvet with his mighty needle."

Francis dragged them toward the door. "Come on, Thomas. There must be something more interesting to do than let Angelo make our ears bleed!"

They burst out of the tavern, singing, into the dark, damp streets.

It was nearly sunrise when Francis went to sleep. He was still excited about his new armor, and dreamed of a large palace with helmets, spears, and shields covering the walls.

Whose are these? he wondered, admiring the shining display.

He saw no one, but heard a voice, clear and confident. "They are destined for you and your knights."

He slept contentedly until midday.

It took several months for Count Gentile to gather his army and provisions. Francis' mother begged him not to go. But he was determined to become the hero the troubadours sang of, and the dream had boosted his confidence. So Francis rode out of Assisi for the second time, splendid in his gleaming chain mail and riding an elegant horse. The caravan wound slowly across the countryside below Assisi, and soon the town had disappeared from their view. It was a long day of riding.

At Spoleto they stopped for the night, and the camp was soon buzzing with disturbing news. "Walter de Brienne has died in battle in Apulia!"

Francis was stunned and suddenly felt exhausted. His head throbbing, he curled under his blanket and began to drift to sleep when he heard someone say, "Where are you going, Francis?"

"Walter's campaign against the Germans must go on," he murmured sleepily. "It's my destiny to become a great knight."

"Who will reward you more for your deeds, the lord or the servant?"

"The lord, of course."

"Then why are you leaving the lord for the servant?"

His head was foggy with sleep. "Who are you? What do you want me to do?"

"Return home, and you will be told. The weapons you saw in your dream are not for you, Francis. Your palace will be far different from what you expect."

He jumped up and peered intently into the dark, but saw only his companions snoring beside the fire. *Was I dreaming? Was the count talking in his sleep?* Francis rolled himself back up in his blanket, but he couldn't get comfortable. *What other kinds of weapons and palaces are there? What is my destiny, if not a life of chivalry?*

All night he tossed and turned, plagued by his doubts. When day broke, he gathered his pack and his weapons and announced that he was going back to Assisi.

"Worthless squire!" Count Gentile spat at him. "I should have known that a skinny, spoiled boy like you wasn't trustworthy. Go home before I send you home in pieces!"

"I didn't quit," Francis explained to his friends when he returned to Assisi so quickly. "Walter is dead. I'll go back when someone worthy takes up his sword."

But he muttered to himself, *Some knight I turned out to be.*

To his father's glad surprise, he spent many hours helping in the shop on the first floor of their house. He waited on customers. He delivered orders to the nobles. He went into the slums and supervised workers dying fabric in big vats.

Peter Bernadone decided that perhaps his son was going to make him proud after all.

In his free hours, Francis wandered the countryside below the town, questioning his destiny. *If I am not to be a knight, what am I to do with my life? Be a cloth merchant like my father?* The idea did not appeal to him.

One morning he stood at the counter in the shop, tallying the price of an order on his father's abacus. Colorful stacks of fine wool and delicate silk spilled out of a row of bins. Peter kept the bins propped off the floor to protect his goods from the rainwater and sewage that ran down from the higher parts of town.

The door creaked open and someone shuffled in. Francis shifted the wooden beads of the abacus and glanced up. "Yes?"

An old man stepped forward into the light, and Francis smelled him before he saw the filthy breeches and the one red, shriveled hand.

"Please, young man. In the name of God, give a poor cripple some food."

Francis jumped up and threw open the door. "Get out of here, old man. This shop is for paying customers, not beggars."

"Please, in the name of God."

"Go!"

The old man hobbled out and Francis slammed the door.

Turning to the abacus again, he suddenly realized how little money it would take to help the beggar. *You'd lend him the money if he was a count*, he thought, *and a crippled old man needs it much more than a count.* He snatched up a pouch of coins and ran out to the street.

The old man was shuffling toward another shop.

"Wait!" Francis called. He ran to the beggar and pressed the pouch into his good hand. "I'm sorry I was so rude. Take this. It will buy you enough bread for a month."

The old man grinned at him with rotten teeth. "God bless you, my son."

Francis went back to the shop. *I'll never again turn away someone who asks for help in God's name*, he promised.

That night at the tavern, he was quiet while his friends sang battle songs.

"Francis is bored," Thomas said, yanking Angelo's fiddle out of his hands. "Let's go steal a horse."

They moved toward the door, but Francis didn't get up.

"Francis! Are you daydreaming?"

"Perhaps he's thinking of a beautiful woman," teased Angelo. "Did you choose a wife and forget to tell us?"

Francis smiled. "I'm going to bring home a bride more beautiful and noble than you can imagine."

His friends laughed and slapped him on the back. "Come on, lover boy."

I used to think Lady Chivalry was my destiny, he thought. *But these days it is Lady Poverty who haunts me. Perhaps the voice I hear in my dreams is God.*

He got to his feet and absently followed his companions out of the tavern.

In the days that followed, he began to spend more time in the fields below the town. His father owned several farms, payments from nobles who purchased his finest fabrics. Francis gladly escaped the stench and closeness of the overcrowded town, wandering in the fresh air through olive groves and wheat fields. The peace and beauty of nature seemed to calm his troubled soul.

Some days Angelo went with him. His friend would sit at the mouth of a small cave and whittle sticks while Francis prayed inside.

"Do you ever get the feeling that God is trying to tell you something?" Francis asked him as they sat on the rocks.

Angelo raised an eyebrow. "Like what?"

"I'm not sure." He looked away. "My possessions seem like a burden, and I wonder if I would be better off without them."

"Is this another of your practical jokes?"

"No, Angelo. Look at those wheat stalks. All they need are the soil, rain, and sun that God gives them. In return, they praise him by growing into beautiful, fruitful fields. So why do we think we need palaces full of swords and tapestries? Why are we not satisfied with the food and shelter God provides?"

"You're serious, aren't you?"

Francis turned to him with earnest eyes. "I think God wants me to do something big, something more noble even than knighthood, if that is possible. I just don't know what it is yet."

One autumn day when Angelo was busy in town, Francis wandered further into the hills than usual. Rounding a clump of cypress trees, he came upon a tiny old chapel, one of many that dotted the Italian countryside. It was crumbling, small piles of broken stone lying where they had tumbled from the walls. An inscription honoring Saint Damiano was almost worn away.

Inside a hedge, Francis could see that someone had scratched out a sparse garden next to a little hut. It was probably a lone priest who tended the chapel. Only the beans had grown with any success.

He slipped into the building, a small sanctuary the only room.

It was cool and dark inside. A cross with flaking paint hung over a low altar. Francis kneeled in the silence. *Lord, I seek your will. If I am not to become a knight, what would you have me do?*

He had lost track of how long he had been praying when he heard a voice. "Francis, don't you see that my house has collapsed? Go and repair it for me."

He glanced behind him, but the chapel was empty. Was God speaking to him again?

"Repair my house, Francis."

Yes, that's it! thought Francis. *Lots of knights sponsor church repairs. These walls need new stones, and the lamps need oil, and the priest could probably use some meat.*

"Yes, Lord, I will willingly repair your house," he said aloud.

There was no answer.

He got to his feet and went outside. A shabby priest was coming through the hedge and looked up at his visitor in surprise.

"Hello!"

"Father Giovanni." Francis recognized him from the market in Assisi.

He quickly reached into his money pouch and pressed several coins into the priest's hand. "Please take this," he said. "Use it to keep the lamps burning and to buy yourself some food."

"The Lord bless you!" said the priest, dazed. "I'm surprised that a young prankster like you would be interested in spiritual things."

"That's just a deposit," Francis promised. "I will be back with more."

He returned to Assisi that night excited about his new quest.

In the morning, he went down to the shop on the first floor and examined his father's inventory. Peter was on another buying trip in France, and Francis wasn't about to wait until he got back to discuss his plan. He gathered up as much of the fine fabric as he could bundle onto a horse, and set out for the nearby town of Foligno. His father had several regular customers there.

It didn't take long to sell everything, including the horse. Francis tied the bursting money bag onto his belt, tucked it into his breeches, and walked back to San Damiano Chapel.

But Father Giovanni refused the money. "The church is no place for practical jokes!"

"No, you don't understand. This is a sincere donation to rebuild San Damiano."

The priest hesitated. "Your father sent you to bring this?"

"No, my father doesn't even know about it. I sold a load of cloth and a horse."

"You stole this money?" demanded Giovanni. He thought, *And worse, you stole it from Peter Bernadone? He's a powerful man!*

"It's my inheritance," Francis insisted. "So it's really my money. And there is a lot here! It will pay for all the necessary repairs."

"I'm sorry, Francis. I can see that your heart is good, but I cannot take this."

"Well, I'm not keeping it!" Francis stomped his foot and tossed the money through a high window. The bag lodged on the crumbling windowsill.

Giovanni shook his head.

I guess money isn't the only thing I have to give, thought Francis. "God told me to repair this church, and I'm going to do it if I have to use my own hands!"

The priest grinned. "That offer I can accept!"

Francis got to work clearing the rubble. Father Giovanni let him stay in his hut, and over the next few days, they erected scaffolding and inspected the broken roof tiles. But his work was soon interrupted by a message from Peter Bernadone.

"Father has returned to Assisi and discovered his missing

inventory!" Francis told the priest in a rush. "He's very angry."

Giovanni shrugged as if to say, *I told you!*

"I need to disappear for awhile," Francis declared. "But I will be back. You have my word as a knight."

For a month, he hid in the cave where he had prayed with Angelo. He felt guilty for promising Giovanni he would repair the chapel and then leaving before the work was done. *If I go back, I'll have to face my father*, he thought. *All he understands is making money. He cannot see the value in giving it away.* Yes, he was convinced now that God was calling him to give away his possessions. *But if I don't go back, I can't complete my quest.* He prayed for guidance.

Finally, he decided to return to Assisi. But he wouldn't go home. He would just ask his friends for food and building supplies, so he could get back to his work at San Damiano. He would do it without his father.

He reached the city gates before nightfall and headed toward the piazza. But the whole town knew his father was looking for him, and Peter had been alerted as soon as Francis came through the gates. He was waiting for him in front of the tavern with some of his men.

"Where have you been?" Peter demanded. "You look like a leper!"

That much was true. He hadn't eaten or bathed in a month. He was filthy, skinny, and his beard had grown long. No wonder people had hurried to get out of his way as he came into town.

Francis stood his ground. "I have been praying and fasting."

"Don't pretend to be a holy man, Francis. You are just a thief and a coward! Is this how you repay me for the ransom I paid when you were so foolish to be captured in battle?"

"Is money all you care about?"

"How can you despise all my years of labor? My grandfather was a serf. I have achieved so much more than he could have hoped for, and look how you squander it!" He waved to his men. "Lock him in my cellar! He will stay there until he repays what he stole!"

They dragged him into the prison and left him in the dark. Memories of the Perugian dungeon came to him in a rush. *Well, this is certainly not a life of luxury*, he told himself. *Lady Poverty would be pleased.*

A few weeks later, Father Giovanni was praying at San Damiano's altar when he heard approaching steps.

"Francis! I didn't expect you to come back. I heard your father had locked you in the family prison!"

"He did," Francis said. "But as soon as he left on another buying trip, my mother let me out. She raised me to listen to God's voice, and I explained all about my desire to give up luxury and help those in need. So I have returned to complete my quest."

Father Giovanni shook his head and smiled. "Your heart is good, but you know this is not over. As soon as your father returns to Assisi, he will come looking for you again."

"Let him come. This time I will not run away."

He took the priest by the arm and led him to a wheelbarrow outside the hedge. "Look what I brought! I spent the last few days begging bricks from the kind people of Assisi. There are enough here to begin rebuilding the walls."

"I don't know what to make of you, Francis," said Giovanni. "You beg not for bread but for stones!"

They spent days digging out the crumbling stones, mixing fresh mortar, and filling in the holes. Giovanni worked on the lower portion of the walls, and Francis worked on the higher levels. From the scaffolding, he could see across the hills to the road leading up to Assisi.

"Ho there!" he called to travelers on the road. "Stop for awhile and help me with this load of bricks!"

But they took one look at the filthy young man shouting at them from the roof of a hovel, and kept going.

One afternoon Francis was wiping the sweat from his brow when he noticed a rider approaching. He began to wave at the man and call out to him. But when he recognized the figure, he drew back.

Peter Bernadone had returned to Assisi and was furious to find that Francis had escaped.

"Get down from there at once!" cried the merchant from his saddle. "It's time to stop this foolishness!"

Francis turned to face him, but did not climb down. "I can't leave until I have completed my quest," he replied.

"Your quest! You still think you are a knight?"

He didn't answer.

"If you really believe in noble ideals, then you understand why I cannot allow you to steal from me just because you are my son."

"I have dedicated myself to the work of the Lord. The church is my authority now, not you."

Father Giovanni peeked his head out of the doorway of the chapel, but they didn't notice him.

"Bishop Guido is a friend of mine, Francis, and he is richer than I am!" shouted Peter. "You do not want me to take my petition to him. He will certainly rule in my favor."

Francis turned back to the wall and hefted a stone into place. "Until the bishop instructs me to stop, I have a chapel to rebuild."

"Then you leave me no choice," Peter cried. "You are a disgrace to the Bernadone name!"

He spun his horse around and galloped away.

The priest looked up at the young man on the scaffold. "You are not a disgrace. You are a knight in monk's clothing."

Within days, Francis was summoned to trial. Giovanni insisted on going with him, and together they set out to climb the ridge toward the city. When they arrived, they were given rooms in the bishop's palace overnight. Francis accepted the offer of a bath, but refused to sleep in the comfortable bed.

The next morning was cold enough that Francis could see his breath. He was surprised to discover a crowd of spectators shivering in Guido's courtyard.

"The whole town knows of this dispute between father and son," said Giovanni with a shrug. "You may not be a knight, but you seem to have found fame anyway."

Francis frowned and took his place before the bishop's couch in the center of the courtyard. Scanning the crowd, he noticed Angelo, who gave him an encouraging smile. But his confidence faded when his father stepped forward. Peter held his powerful chin high and said not a word to his son.

Bishop Guido rose from his couch and called the people to order. He was a large man, and Francis noticed that under his heavy cloak he was dressed in Peter's finest linen.

"This trial shall begin," the bishop declared in a booming voice. "Peter Bernadone, state your complaint."

The merchant ignored the crowd and spoke directly to Guido. "My son Francis stole from me a horse and goods from my shop."

"You asked him to return them?"

"He refuses to repay his debt. I have appealed to this court because he claims the church's authority."

Guido gestured to Francis with a heavy hand covered in rings. "Is this true, young man?"

He stepped forward. "I did sell goods from my father's shop, yes. But I did not keep the money for myself. I gave it to Father Giovanni to rebuild the chapel of San Damiano." He nodded at the priest standing at the front of the crowd.

Peter rolled his eyes. "Charity does not justify thievery!"

"Better that the money go to the Lord's work rather than be lost in your giant coffers," retorted Francis.

Peter's face flushed red. "I have spent years building an honest reputation. But you reject my hard work and bring shame to our family!"

"Is it shameful to help the poor?" cried Francis. "Is it shameful to follow Christ? Our Lord told the young nobleman to give away all his possessions. He told his disciples not to carry extra supplies on their journeys. He said whoever would follow him must deny himself!"

"You hide behind the holy Scriptures to justify your actions!"

"Enough!" boomed Bishop Guido. "I have heard enough."

The crowd grew quiet. Guido lowered himself onto his couch. "You have rightly devoted yourself to Christ, Francis. And your generosity toward the poor is commendable." He paused. "But the cloth and the horse you sold belonged to your father. You cannot give to the Lord what is not yours to begin with. He will not honor works done in his name if you have broken his commandments to perform them."

Francis hung his head in shame. "I had not thought of it that way," he mumbled.

"If you wish to serve the Lord, you must return to your father everything you have taken."

Francis looked at Bishop Guido's serious face, at Father Giovanni's threadbare tunic, at Peter Bernadone's soft cloak and leather shoes.

"Then I will restore what I have taken," he said suddenly. "Wait here." He marched into the bishop's garden on the far side of the courtyard.

Winter had stripped the leaves from the shrubs. Francis cupped a bare branch in his cold hands and stroked it tenderly. "You don't complain about giving up your lush green companions, do you? You just glorify God in your loneliness and wait patiently for spring to arrive."

He stepped into an alcove and removed his multi-colored cloak, now gray with dirt. Shivering, he removed the leather belt, the linen tunic, and the finely-woven breeches. He folded each one, stacking them neatly into a pile, and put his money bag on top.

When he stepped back into the courtyard, he was naked, carrying the stack of clothing in front of him.

"What on earth!" Peter sputtered. "Have you completely lost your mind, Francis?"

The young man pushed the pile of clothes into his father's hands. "You are all my witnesses," he yelled to the crowd. "I have returned every last item I ever received from Peter Bernadone. From this point on, my father is in heaven, not in Assisi!"

Bishop Guido rushed forward, removing his white mantle from his shoulders, and wrapped it around Francis. "Trust in the Lord, my son, and he will provide you with all you need."

"I do trust him," replied Francis. "And here and now, I vow to devote my life to rebuilding his church—both the buildings of worship and the hearts of men."

He tied the bishop's mantle around his waist and strode decisively out of the courtyard.

Peter Bernadone stared after him, the stack of clothing in his arms.

"Peace be with you, bishop," mumbled Father Giovanni with a nod, and ran to catch up with Francis.

"Sir Francis has chosen his quest," declared Angelo, pushing through the crowd, "and so have I!" He pushed up his sleeves and went after them.

Astonished, the spectators watched open-mouthed as the half-dressed young man and his two followers marched out the gates of Assisi and into the quiet countryside beyond.

Francis became a troubadour for Lady Poverty, writing songs and poems about how God provided for all of his creation. He soon had many followers. They vowed to beg for everything they needed, and tried to convince wealthy clergy to give their goods to the poor. Eventually the pope granted them permission to found a new order of monks, which became known as the Franciscans.

Francis died in 1226, after suffering for many years from diseases caused by his rigorous lifestyle.

H⊕w the University was B⊕rn

FOR THOUSANDS OF years, people have gathered in communities centered around teaching and learning. The early church formed schools to train Christians in philosophy and theology. One of the most famous early schools was in Alexandria and was led by the church fathers Clement and Origen. These schools are sometimes referred to as *universities*, but universities as we know them did not begin until the Middle Ages.

In many ways, the story begins with Emperor Charlemagne (742-814), who made education a priority of his empire. The social reforms he began had such lasting effects that we call his reign the *Carolingian renaissance*. With his support, many new monasteries were formed to train monks about the Bible. He hired scholars to teach at these monasteries. Some cathedrals also started schools. It was natural to find monks wherever a school was founded.

One of the major contributions of these schools are the biblical manuscripts they copied in beautiful *calligraphy*. Because the printing press had not yet been invented, they had to copy books by hand. Today we still have many of these pages, some with ornate color illustrations. These are known as *illuminated manuscripts*.

Education had always been a privilege of the wealthy. But the educational reforms of Charlemagne created opportunities for the less fortunate. When the poorest families could not afford to feed their children, they could give their sons to the monasteries. The monks would provide food and shelter for the boys, and teach them how to read and copy books.

The cathedral and monastery schools provided a basic education in literature and church doctrine. But advanced training in other disciplines was needed, too. A medical school was founded in Salerno. A law school in Bologna came under the protection of Emperor Frederick Barbarossa in 1158, and was later recognized as a formal university.

By 1200, the university in Paris had become the center for teaching logic and theology. It was here that famous theologians like Thomas Aquinas (1225-1274) earned their reputations. Later in the century, universities in Oxford and Cambridge were modeled after the Paris school. Soon there were universities in Prague, Vienna, Cologne, and in Muslim territories.

The average university student was much younger than today. Children were educated at home until they were about fourteen. Then the brighter boys were sent to the university for further studies.

Girls were not allowed to attend university. Most of them married. Some decided not to marry, and instead dedicated themselves to the service of the church, joining *convents*, or monasteries for women. They ate and slept in the convents, continued their studies there, and spent their days praying, feeding the poor, and nursing sick people.

As *bachelors* in the universities, the boys studied seven subjects. The first three, called the *trivium*, were grammar, rhetoric, and logic. These subjects prepared students for advanced studies in the *quadrivium* of arithmetic, geometry, music, and astronomy. Then they studied philosophy, theology, or medicine. When they completed their studies, they were given the title of *master*, which gave them the right to teach in the university. If they chose to continue their education, they earned the title *doctor*. Today we recognize similar levels of education by granting *bachelor's* degrees, *master's* degrees, and *doctoral* degrees.

The Middle Ages are often called the *Dark Ages*, an unfortunate nickname that suggests people were barbaric, uneducated, and superstitious. But the birth of universities and the development of illuminated manuscripts proves that education and the arts were alive and well during the Medieval period.

Thomas Aquinas: We call him the Dumb Ox

1248. COLOGNE, GERMANY.

EVERY MORNING WHEN he stepped into the library, Thomas drew a deep breath. The air in this chamber was different from the rest of the cathedral. He savored the strong acidity of fresh ink, the must of yellowed pages. The mingled scents always drew him toward the stacks of books. Some were centuries old. Others had been hand-copied only days ago.

The library was part of his morning ritual. Every day except Sunday, he rose before dawn, buckled a leather belt around his white tunic, and—if it was cold—pulled a black hooded robe over his head. He emptied his chamber pot into the chute at the end of the corridor, returned the pot to its place under his bed, and tucked the wool blanket under the corners of his straw mattress. Then he joined his fellow students in the refectory for the morning lecture with Master Albert. It lasted about two hours. Then they moved to the long, narrow tables against the wall and chanted a prayer together. Bowls of hot porridge were distributed and eaten in silence. When the schoolmaster dismissed them,

Thomas always went directly to the library.

Now, he hunched his large frame to see the leather-bound volumes on the bottom shelf. When he found the one he was looking for, he carried it to a table under a window. The book was nearly the size of the small tabletop.

By this time, the sun had risen well above the adjacent rooftops. He settled himself in a shaft of sunlight under the window and began to read, following the text with his index finger. From time to time he scrawled notes in a small notebook he fished from the pocket dangling from his belt.

"That's a rather sophisticated argument, don't you think?"

He left the finger on the page to mark his place and slowly raised his eyes. He had been so absorbed in the reading, he hadn't heard the man approach. It was a fellow student, leaning on the edge of the table, smiling.

"What?"

"The book. You've been reading it for hours. You missed the afternoon meal."

Startled, he glanced at the window. The sun had passed its highest point and was just beginning to descend. "That means I only have a few minutes before the next lecture! I guess I lost track of time."

The man laughed and stuck out a knobby hand. "I'm William."

"Hi, I'm Thomas."

"Yes, I know who you are. The big Italian who never says anything in class."

Thomas leaned back on his stool. "That's a nicer way of putting it than what people usually call me."

"The 'Dumb Ox'? There's nothing wrong with being quiet. The students are just used to everyone here arguing with the lecturers to prove how smart they are. Plus, they've never seen a Dominican friar with the shoulders of a blacksmith!" He dragged a second chair under the window and sat. "Anyway, maybe I can help you. I'm a tutor here. I'd be glad to assist you with your studies." He smiled.

"Oh! Uh, well, thank you. But there is no need—."

"No obligation. Just as a friend. Really, I'd be glad to."

He's so eager, it would be rude to send him away, thought Thomas. "I'm honored by your offer," he said. "Thank you."

"Great! We can start with this book. Master Albert assigned the reading?"

"Yes."

"Let's see where you are." He leaned across the book and read past Thomas' finger.

"Now I see why you were concentrating so hard. This section is a challenge for the brightest student!"

Thomas nodded politely.

"I love this argument. The logic is so intricate, so careful. Let me see if I can explain it." He glanced at the page again, tapping a finger on the table. Thomas waited. William cleared his throat. "Actually, it would be hard to just jump in and explain. We should start a bit earlier in the text." He fiddled with the large pages.

"Perhaps I could try explaining it to you and you can correct me where I am wrong?" prompted Thomas.

William pushed the book aside with relief and smiled. "Yes, good idea. Go ahead."

Thomas began to lay out the writer's argument, speaking slowly and carefully. William leaned forward, stunned at the clarity of the young man's logic. *He's doing more than summarizing the book, he's pointing out the logical flaws. He says it so hesitantly, like he's unsure of himself, but every word he uses is precise, exact. What have I gotten myself into?*

"But perhaps I misunderstood the author," Thomas was saying. "What do you think?"

"I think *you* should tutor *me*," William whispered.

"I'm sorry! I was out of line to speak for so long to a senior student."

"No, that's not what I mean," insisted William. "I mean, you've been holding out on us with your silent routine! You just explained this topic to me more clearly than I've ever heard. I want you to be my tutor."

Thomas scooted his chair back, hands raised. "No, no. You have earned your position here. I don't want to damage your reputation."

"A scholar who puts his reputation over scholarship doesn't deserve to be a tutor. Humility is as desirable as knowledge."

"Well——." Thomas scratched his head and then stuck out his big hand again. "Okay, I'll do it, but don't tell anyone."

"Don't tell anyone what?" asked a voice behind them.

"Master Albert!"

The schoolmaster stood between the stacks, his hands clasped loosely in front of him. He raised an eyebrow and peered at them over his long nose. "Are you two up to something?"

"No, Master Albert," said Thomas, respectfully lowering his gaze. "William is tutoring me in the reading you assigned."

The lecturer nodded. "Good! Maybe he can also teach you to speak up in class."

"Yes, Master Albert," said William.

"And Thomas, you are not permitted to skip meals to study. If you need help with your assignments, you will seek it from William or one of the other tutors—but not during prayer or meal times."

"Yes, Master Albert."

"I'll see you both at my next lecture in a few minutes."

William grinned at Thomas as soon as he was gone. "Yeah, you dumb ox. You know you can come to me when you need help."

"I'm sure I will learn a lot from you as we study together," insisted Thomas.

William laughed at him again and stood. "Can we meet tomorrow? I started writing a treatise on logic and I'd like you to read it."

"Okay."

They collected their books and parted.

Thomas lumbered down the long corridor and went out a side exit into the wide, rectangular courtyard. The air outside was warmer than he expected, and fresher than inside the damp stone buildings. His stomach rumbled, complaining about the missed meal. *But I did make a new friend*, he told himself, *and the reading was quite interesting*.

A pair of ducks paddled across the sparkling surface of the fish pond at the center of the yard. He lingered, watching them, feeling the sun on his face.

Master Albert may not think much of me, but it is a privilege to study under him at the cathedral school. He settled himself on the low retaining wall of the pool, his long legs pressed against his chest. A leaf stirred by the breeze *plinked* into the water and disturbed his glassy reflection.

Sometimes I can't believe I'm really here after everything it took to make it happen. Wasn't I only five years old when my parents dedicated me to a different future?

"I don't want to go to Monte Cassino," the boy had told his mother when he found out they were sending him to live at the monastery there. "I want to stay with you."

Theodora, his mother, firmly shut the lid of the trunk she was packing. "You cannot become the abbot of Monte Cassino if you stay here."

"But I don't want to be an abbot. I want to be a knight like my father and my brother Rinaldo."

"The abbey is a respectable future, my son," she said, taking him gently by the shoulders. "And being a knight is not all swordplay!

It's because of your father's position as one of Emperor Frederick's knights that you must go to Monte Cassino. I know you don't understand this yet, but the emperor is finally at peace with the pope—at least for now—and that means your father needs to build a good relationship with the church. You will get a fine education at the monastery and make your father proud." She kissed his forehead.

The day Thomas set out from the family castle in Roccasecca, he was accompanied by his father, Sir Landulf of Aquino, and a host of his father's men. Thomas rode the whole way in silence. His father had been away in battle so much, the boy thought of him as a stranger. Usually when they were together, Landulf said little to him, but on this trip, he was reassuring.

"Monte Cassino has a great heritage, Thomas," said the knight. "It was founded by Benedict of Nursia, who built monasteries all over Italy. It stands high on a mountain for all the world to see. It used to be a military fortress, you know."

Thomas didn't respond.

Landulf dropped his voice to a whisper, like he was telling a secret. "They say that before he captured Rome, the barbarian King Totila came to visit Benedict at this monastery."

Thomas continued to stare at the seat across the carriage.

Landulf took the boy by the chin and looked into his eyes. "You're going to receive a great education here and someday become the abbot. Make your father proud, Thomas."

From the way his parents had described Monte Cassino, Thomas pictured a glorious castle on the mountaintop, hedged by lush gardens and fields. But as they approached, he discovered that the monastery had served as a fort during Emperor Frederick's recent struggle with the pope. The old building had been damaged, and the fields were full of rocks, brambles, and broken-down windmills.

But the abbot who greeted them was friendly. "You're taller

than I expected, but you must be Thomas," he said, reaching for the boy's hand. "Welcome to Monte Cassino."

Thomas spent nearly nine years there.

He was surprised to discover that he loved books. He hurried through his chores—planting grain in the fields, scrubbing the cobblestones, carrying water to the monk's rooms—so he could sneak into the scriptorium and watch the monks copy books. The abbot quickly recognized that his young helper was bright. By the time he was fourteen, Thomas had nearly decided to dedicate his life to the monastery.

But something happened before he could take the solemn vow. Emperor Frederick declared war against the pope again. The pope excommunicated the emperor from the church of Rome. So Frederick expelled all the pope's supporters from his territories.

For safety, the abbot sent Thomas to Naples to study at the brand new university founded by the emperor.

His first day there, he noticed several men wearing black wool cloaks. As they made their way toward the cathedral, people paused on the street to hand them loaves of bread and vegetables. The men raised their hands in blessing and tucked the offerings into their robes.

Those beggars are monks, he noted with surprise. But they wore black cloaks instead of the brown camel-hair ones typical of the Benedictines. And the Benedictines at Monte Cassino never begged. They grew their own vegetables and baked their own bread. They even provided for the poorest people in the nearby villages. He had never seen a monk ask someone to provide for him.

"Excuse me," said Thomas, stopping a man coming toward him. "Who are those men over there?"

The man looked in the direction he was pointing. "Those are Dominican monks. Have you never heard of them?"

"I've heard of them, but I've never seen them."

"They are an order of preachers active in the university, as students and teachers. They were founded not even a hundred years ago by a teacher named Dominic."

Thomas thanked him for the information and set out to find the university.

He had been in Naples for only a few days when he met one of the Dominican preachers. Friar John was from San Giuliano. He taught at the university and at the cathedral, a popular teacher in both places. When he spoke, he often closed his eyes, clasped his hands behind his back, and rocked slightly on his feet. Thomas found his lectures fascinating.

Sometimes after teaching at the university, Friar John would invite Thomas to walk back with him to the cathedral. They were an unlikely pair, the slight preacher in his black cap and cloak and the stocky teenager in his camel-hair robe. The friar did most of the talking. Thomas just listened.

"You're a humble man," the preacher observed one afternoon. "Eager to learn, but not eager to speak. Tell me, Thomas. What do you think of the Dominicans?"

Thomas hesitated. "I guess I am surprised to find monks so interested in the university. You are as dedicated to teaching as bishops, but unlike them, you are not bound to one congregation."

John smiled. "We Dominicans honor education, and teach wherever we go. Your Benedictine abbot was not a man of learning?"

"It's not that the Benedictines don't see the value of knowledge. My abbot made sure I received a basic education at Monte Cassino." He paused. "But they don't travel around for the sake of teaching. They find it more important to separate themselves from the world so they can concentrate on prayer."

"No one can spend enough time in prayer," agreed John. "They are right to emphasize that. But if every man of prayer locks himself away all the time, who is there to teach others to pray?"

Thomas thought about this. "The Benedictines give to the poor. But you Dominicans ask the poor to give to you. Why do you beg for your food instead of work for it?"

"Like you said, prayer is the key to the Christian life. We believe that God wants us to rely on him for all that we need. So we ask God to provide our food and shelter, and then we ask his people to share with us the blessings he has given them."

Thomas was even more quiet the rest of the way home.

After months of listening to Friar John, he finally decided he did not want to dedicate himself to the Benedictine order after all. But he didn't know what he was going to do instead. John encouraged him to consider joining the Dominicans and become a teacher, but Thomas knew it would upset his parents. The Dominicans were loyal to the pope, not to Emperor Frederick. Besides, no wealthy family wanted a beggar for a son.

Then came a conversation that changed his life for good.

"Thomas!" called Friar John, hailing him on the steps outside the cathedral. "Thomas, a wonderful opportunity has come up. The master general, John of Wildeshausen, has arrived in Naples. I want you to meet him."

Thomas wasn't sure what to say. "I haven't decided yet if I should join the Dominicans. I want to, but I'm not willing to dishonor my parents."

"I know," said John. "Wealthy and important families usually object to their sons joining our order. But that is not enough of a reason to reject us. And things usually have a way of working themselves out with parents."

"I need more time to decide."

"I'm sorry," John said. "But the master general won't be in the area for long. If you don't decide now, it may be a long time before you have the chance again."

"What happens if I decide to join?"

"I have told him about you, and he is anxious to meet you," said John. "He'll take you to Paris to continue your education."

"I'd have to leave my studies here?"

"Paris is the best theology school in the world!"

"But I'm only nineteen. Don't I have to be older to join the order?"

"The Dominicans don't accept anyone under eighteen."

Thomas looked at his friend. He had run out of excuses, and it sounded exciting. "Okay," he agreed finally. "Take me to meet the master general."

John of Wildeshausen liked Thomas immediately. Within days they left for Paris on horseback, planning to stop in Bologna on the way. But thunderstorms slowed their progress. Heavy rains spattered off the trees and dug rivulets in the road. They were soon cold, wet, and coated with mud.

"Maybe we should stop and wait for the storm to pass," shouted one of their companions.

"No," insisted the master general. "It will soon be dark, and the road will be more dangerous. There is a town not far ahead where we can stop for the night."

They urged the horses to go faster. The daylight began to fade, and the woods grew denser as they entered the valley. In the gray mist below the trees suddenly appeared a band of men.

Thomas' horse reared in surprise and tossed him into the mud.

"What is this?" shouted the master general.

Swords rang out of their sheaths. The Dominicans found the blades pointed at their necks.

"Nobody move," someone growled.

A bulky figure shouldered his way past the line of marauders and stooped over Thomas in the mud.

Sheets of drizzle were still falling and the sky had grown dark. Thomas couldn't make out the man's face.

"You are Thomas?"

"Leave him alone!" cried the master general. He struggled to free himself, but the raiders forced him to the ground.

"This is the one we want," said the leader. "His family will pay a high price for his ransom." With a grunt, he pulled Thomas to his feet.

"Don't hurt them," Thomas said quietly. "I'll come with you if you promise not to harm my brothers."

The leader clutched at Thomas' black cloak. "First you'll take off that disgraceful robe!"

"This is a symbol of my dedication to the Dominicans. I will not remove it."

They tried to pry it off him, but he shoved them away.

"Forget it," ordered the leader. "I don't want him injured." He shoved Thomas toward his horse. "Get on the horse."

"I'll walk."

"Don't try to slow us down. Get on the horse!" His hand was still on his sword.

Thomas climbed back on his horse and turned to his companions in the dark. "God be with you, brothers!"

He was forced into the woods.

They rode well into the night. For hours, no one spoke. Finally, Thomas insisted on knowing where they were taking him.

"Roccasecca," was the answer.

Roccasecca! "Who is behind this?" he demanded.

"Quiet!" they growled at him.

The sky was just beginning to lighten again when they approached a castle. Thomas was dismayed to make out a flag bearing his grandfather's crest.

"This is my mother's castle!" He cut off the leader's horse, forcing him to stop. "Who are you?"

The man threw back his deep hood. It was his brother Rinaldo.

"Why are you doing this?" cried Thomas.

"You're a disgrace to your family! Take him to the tower."

They dragged him, soaked with rain and mud, into the castle.

He was sleeping on the stone floor when the scraping of a lock woke him. It had been several years since he had seen his mother. Theodora's face was slightly fuller and the hair around her temples lighter, but she still had the proud bearing of her Norman ancestors.

"I did not expect to see you next under such conditions," she said from the door.

"Nor did I!"

She took a step forward. "How could you do this to your family, Thomas?"

"Me? You sent my own brother to kidnap me!"

"He was the only one I could trust to stop you."

He looked away, unwilling to see the disappointment on her face. "I haven't done anything except devote myself to prayer and study. You're the one who wanted me to become a monk."

"A Benedictine monk," corrected Theodora. "Not a Dominican! They are loyal to the pope, and the pope is Frederick's enemy."

"At the moment! But Frederick changes his mind every day. Anyway, that doesn't matter. I believe in their mission."

"There is much more at stake than what you believe. Your first duty is to your family."

"Respectfully, mother, you are wrong. My first duty is to my conscience."

"You will not leave here until you agree to abandon the order."

He folded his arms across the black robe and refused to say anything more.

"Get him some dry clothes and food," she demanded as she swept out the door. The key turned again in the lock.

When the clothes were tossed into the cell, he gladly changed into dry trousers and a clean tunic, but immediately pulled the muddy robe over them.

He was imprisoned in the tower for months. When the master general discovered who was behind the kidnapping, he petitioned the pope to secure Thomas' release. But the castle was in Frederick's territory, and he refused to entertain pleas, especially from the pope.

All of his brothers and sisters came to convince Thomas to leave the Dominicans. His sister Marotta visited him in his cell every day. He hadn't seen her since she was a little girl. She looked a lot like their mother now. Her tone was angry, but she brought him extra food and books.

"Don't you see how hard this is on all of us?" she pouted. "Would it really be so terrible to join the Benedictines instead and get back to your studies in peace?"

"I have committed myself to the Dominican cause," insisted Thomas, shaking his head. "They love education but they don't keep it to themselves. They go from town to town preaching the Scripture to all who will listen."

"But, Thomas, you have to beg for your living!" Her dark eyes were wide with disbelief.

His voice was gentle. "Jesus told us not to worry about tomorrow. By begging each day for only what I need that day, I can concentrate on living that day in a manner that pleases God."

"But you'll lose mother's support!"

"You're not hearing me," said Thomas tenderly. "I don't need her money. God supplies for me wherever I go through his faithful servants who share whatever I need."

She saw the sincerity on his face. "You are really free from the cares of this world, aren't you?"

"Yes, sister, I am. I only wish I could make our mother see that."

"Give her time," said Marotta. "She is stubborn, but she will not hold you here forever."

Rinaldo came to see Thomas, too. First he offered him money to leave the Dominican order. When that didn't work, he threatened his brother.

"What more can you do to me?" Thomas shrugged in response. "I'm already a prisoner in my own castle."

He spent most of his time reading the Bible and writing in his notebooks. Eventually, his mother gave in and allowed some of his Dominican friends to visit him in the tower. But she refused to release him.

One day Marotta told her brother she had decided to join him. "I want to dedicate my life to God like you have," she said. "And some of our brothers and cousins are beginning to think this way as well. It seems your time here has been profitable after all."

"I'm so glad to hear it!" he said, taking her hand. "I will pray for you. Mother will not be happy."

Theodora arrived at the door soon after Marotta left.

"I suppose you have heard your sister's news already," she said accusingly.

He nodded.

"It appears your presence here has hurt Frederick's cause more than it has helped."

"I'm sorry, mother," said Thomas. "I do not mean to hurt our family's reputation or security with the emperor. I am simply doing what I believe is right."

"And now your sister has taken up your cause. She intends to join a Dominican convent instead of marrying the knight I have chosen for her."

Thomas decided it was best not to respond.

She went to him and put her hand on his arm. He was almost

twice her size. "You have changed so much since we sent you to Monte Cassino, Thomas. You're much taller and stronger and more educated." She sighed. "But you're just as stubborn. I've only ever wanted what is best for you and for this family. You know that I love you."

"I know, mother."

"You resisted me at five and you continue to resist me at twenty. I can see I will never convince you, so I might as well let you go." She looked up at him with tearful eyes. "You're free to go. But you are on your own now. If you choose to side with the pope over the emperor, your family will never support you."

"I understand," he said, kissing the top of her head. "God be with you, mother."

Immediately, he set out for Paris with his friends, who were overjoyed at his release. The master general happily introduced him to a professor named Albert. Master Albert thought him odd and unusually quiet, but he liked him, and invited him to go to the school in Cologne with him.

And now he found himself sitting in the cathedral courtyard in Cologne, staring at the broad forehead and wide shoulders reflected back at him from the fishpond. *Was all that worth going through to get here?* he wondered.

The reflection nodded, *yes*.

Then forget your family's reputation. Forget what the other students call you. Seek Master Albert's direction. Use your mind for the glory of God and you will have fulfilled your purpose.

Master Albert! "I'm going to be late for his lecture," he mumbled aloud. He pulled himself to his feet and headed for the arches on the far side of the courtyard. He didn't notice he had left his notebook beside the pool.

The breeze was ruffling the pages when William came by a few minutes later. He was going to be late, too, but he snatched up the book when he saw it. *This belongs to Thomas*, he thought. *I'd better take it with me.*

Rushing down the corridor toward the refectory, he glanced through the pages. He was so amazed at what he read that he stopped walking, his face buried in the book.

"What are you doing out here, William?" called Master Albert, passing him in the corridor. "You will be late for my lecture."

He looked up in surprise. "Sorry, sir."

"What are you reading?"

"It's Thomas' notebook. He left it out by the pond."

The schoolmaster held out his hand. "I'll see that it is returned."

"Yes, Master Albert," said William, handing it over. "But you might want to read a little of it first."

The schoolmaster leafed through the pages, stopped, turned a few more pages, and stopped again. "Well, I see what you mean," he said. "His handwriting is almost impossible to read! But these conclusions are astonishing."

"He's a genius!" declared William.

"We call him the Dumb Ox," said the schoolmaster, grinning, "but I have a feeling that the bellowing of this ox will one day resound throughout the whole world! I think I'll read a little more of this before I give it back."

He clapped a hand on William's shoulder and they went to meet Thomas in the refectory.

Thomas became a lecturer at the university in Paris and traveled to various cities teaching theology. He wrote a set of books called the Summa Theologica *that became standard textbooks in the church. No theologian since Augustine had as much influence on the church as Thomas did. He died on March 7, 1274, and is still a controversial figure.*

CATHERINE OF SIENNA: DO THAT WHICH YOU HAVE PROMISED

SPRING 1376. FLORENCE, ITALY.

THE CITY OF Florence began as a port on the Arno River. Narrow houses and docks sprang up along both banks of the waterway, with a series of wooden bridges to connect them. Wool dyers, weavers, and embroiderers produced fine textiles to export to other regions of Italy. As the port became prosperous, lavish homes and soaring cathedrals were added to the skyline. For a thousand years, citizens crossed the famous bridges every day to buy bread, work in the dye houses, or go to church. Now the bridges were just the dried-up bones of the carcass that used to be Florence.

A woman peered into the broken window of a shirtmaker's shop, careful not to catch her long white scarf on the glass shards. The shop was empty except for a heavy workbench in the center.

"There's not even a needle in there," she said with dismay. "Most of the other shops are empty, too, or have nothing worth buying."

"It's not the city I used to know, Catherine," said the man beside her. "First the Black Death, and now the war with Pope Gregory! Before the plague, this street was full of merchants at this time of day."

He pointed ahead to the tower rising above the jumble of houses. "Keep walking toward the palace. That is where we are to meet them."

She moved on, keeping stride with her tall friend. Both wore black cloaks. A cluster of women dressed in black with white head coverings followed them up the hill.

"Why have the Florentines not made peace with the pope?" she asked. "Surely they want to end the war."

"The Anti-papal League has barely been able to keep mercenaries from burning down the city," he said. "They have no time to pursue lengthy peace talks in Avignon."

She stopped again and turned to him with a sudden intensity. Her black eyes glowed like coals in her pale face. "Raymond, do *you* believe the pope is at fault in this war?"

He shook his head. "My dear Catherine, I am your confessor, not the other way around! It is not my place to question the motives of the pope."

"Still," she said, returning to her walk, "it sounds as if you're not sure which side to blame."

"I certainly blame those responsible for informing the pope of the conditions here. If he ruled from Rome, instead of Avignon, he would be much closer to what is happening in Florence."

She sighed. "He has said he would restore the papacy to Rome, but so far he has not done it. If we could convince him to come see this for himself . . ." Her voice trailed off.

"I admit that I am also uneasy about these Florentine leaders."

A child darted out of an alley and tugged on her robe, whining for food. She pressed what was left of her lunch into the child's hand. "Share this with your brothers and sisters," she said.

He threw his skinny arms around her and dashed off with the bread.

"Where are his parents?" she said to Raymond as they continued past the crumbling houses.

"They were probably captured as slaves," he said sadly. "The pope's interdict against the city removed all the usual protections. Anyone with a weapon can come in and take whatever he wants. Many of the citizens who survived the Black Death have been carried away as slaves."

"How does that serve the pope's purpose?"

He shrugged his thin shoulders. "Gregory hopes it will force them to give up their rebellion. But I think it only makes them more angry."

The brick bell tower loomed closer. "See the red flag that says *Liberty*?" He pointed. "That is the palace of the Council of Eight. It has a wonderful piazza where the people gather—well, at least they *used* to gather there."

"And all the decisions are made by the Council of Eight?"

"Yes. The council members are citizens who act on behalf of the Anti-papal League."

"The Anti-papal League." She scowled. "What an un-Christian name!"

"Your training tells you it is ungodly to reject the pope, but your heart tells you that someone must help the people of Florence. The well of compassion in you runs deep."

"But only the pope can change these conditions. Somehow we must find a way to help the government reach an agreement with him and end the war for good."

He nodded vigorously. "Your meeting with the Council of Eight is a good start."

She hailed a group of men heading their way. "That must be our welcome party," she said.

He leaned closer to her and lowered his voice. "If they want you to take up their cause with the pope, force them to be honest with you."

She flashed her black eyes at him. "I *always* insist on the truth."

The welcome party led the small caravan to the palace. Catherine and Raymond did not have to wait long for their appointment. They were soon shown into a meeting chamber with a crescent-shaped table and a few rows of chairs. They took the center seats and faced the council.

There were more than eight men behind the table. One of them stood.

"Welcome, Sister Catherine of Sienna and Brother Raymond of Capua," he began. "I am Chancellor Coluccio Salutati. We are the council that runs Florence and the fight for freedom from the pope."

She nodded. "I was glad to receive your invitation. I want to do anything I can to restore Florence's unity with the church."

"The council believes you can influence the pope to end the war."

"First I must understand your position. May I start with a question?"

"Of course." He took his seat.

"What are you trying to achieve with this war? You call it a fight for freedom, but the pope calls it a rebellion."

Chancellor Salutati jumped back to his feet. "If overthrowing the wicked leaders imposed by the pope is a rebellion, then I am happy to agree with him!" he shouted.

She blinked at his sudden outburst.

"Pardon the chancellor," said one of the other council members. "We don't mean to offend you. War and famine have made us bitter."

"Do not make excuses for our position!" retorted the chancellor.

"The pope's leaders take all of our food, money, and land. They accept bribes against the innocent! They care only for their own stomachs, not the people of Italy!"

Catherine raised a delicate hand. "Please, chancellor. I assure you I want to hear your side of the story. There is no need to begin a debate here."

He took a deep breath and sat down again. "Of course. My apologies, sister. Sometimes I get a bit passionate."

"I think we've established that."

"Let me start over. The truth is simple. We refuse to be governed by corrupt leaders. The pope has tried to bully us into submitting to him by cutting us off from supplies and protection. If he does not remove his interdict against this city, the rest of our people are going to die!"

Raymond spoke for the first time. "It may be hard to convince the Holy Father to do that, as long as you are killing his soldiers."

Salutati glared at him, but stayed in his seat. "Listen to me, friends," he said. "Our men are being carried into slavery, while the pope adds towers to his palace. Our women are defending their families with the sword, while the pope finds another chamberlain to dress him. Our children are starving, while the pope complains that his master of the buttery brought him the wrong table knife!"

Catherine looked away, clasping and unclasping her hands in her lap. "I, too, believe that many Christians live more luxuriously than they should," she said finally. "After all, I have chosen to be a Dominican. I beg for my food. But the pope is God's representative on earth! How can we rebel against him?"

"If he is responsible for the deaths of our people, how can we not?"

"Do you really believe bloodshed is the way to reform the church?"

He didn't answer.

"If I can convince him to remove the interdict, are you willing to work toward a compromise?"

"We are willing to discuss it," he agreed, "but we will not go back to the unjust system of before!"

"Then I will help you." She leaned forward. "But you must let me do the talking. Pope Gregory will listen to me, but angry men with swords will not help the peace process."

"We will not attack unless provoked. I assure you, we only want peace and freedom for the people of Florence."

She smiled. "I'm glad to hear it."

"And I am glad you will speak for us. The council has heard amazing stories about you. People say you can work miracles."

"Do not believe everything you hear," she said, rising. "But do pray for a miracle. Only God can resolve the crisis of Florence."

At the door, she turned back to the council. "Before we go to the pope, I would like for my sisters and I to visit with the people. Perhaps we can give them a hand."

He bowed. "Every door in Florence is open to you."

"Thank you."

Catherine took the women traveling with her and walked through the city, looking for people who needed their care. They gathered firewood, boiled broth, swept out houses, tended gardens, fed babies, changed bandages, and prayed with the sick. "I will do everything I can to help the pope understand your plight," she told them.

Salutati appointed several ambassadors to go with them when they set out to meet the pope in the French city of Avignon. The journey took them through the Alps. On the last night, they stopped at a quiet inn. When the proprietor saw that Dominican sisters were part of the caravan, he offered them free rooms and a hot meal.

Catherine took the opportunity to write another letter to the pope. She had written five times already. None of the responses was satisfying. He was willing to meet with her, he said, but he wouldn't promise to grant her request. *I am sure I can convince him once we meet face to face*, she thought.

She sealed the letter and joined Raymond at a table in a corner of the inn. A warm fire blazed in the large fireplace on the far wall, and several of their fellow travelers were seated in front of it.

"I do not trust these ambassadors," he said, glancing at the men around the fire.

"They have promised to follow my lead in this matter," she reminded him.

He lowered his voice. "How do we know they don't have another reason for coming with us?"

"They have given me their word. What good is their word if they can't keep it?"

"And yet they huddle by the fire as though they are plotting!"

She chuckled. "And here we are in the corner, whispering about them. Maybe we are the ones who shouldn't be trusted!"

He frowned at her. "No, they are very angry about the way they feel they've been treated. I do understand that. But I don't think they are ready for peace."

"But who is, Raymond?" she said patiently. "We are all sinners. By nature we are at war with the flesh. Only Christ can bring peace."

"Then I pray that Christ will send his spirit of peace on ahead of us. Tomorrow we shall be in Avignon."

They left early the next morning. By midday, the city was within view. Perched on a rocky hillside, the thick walls snaked down to the banks of the Rhone River. Before the popes had moved the papal residence to Avignon, the houses and shops of the butchers, goldsmiths, bookbinders, and bankers made up most of the city. But for seventy-five years, the popes had been building additions to the papal palace. Now the pope's offices, towers, chapels, and guest houses took up nearly half of the cramped city.

Catherine's caravan was welcomed into the palace. Raymond went to the Dominican monastery. Catherine and the other sisters were given cots in the women's cloister.

She did not sleep well that night. Lying on her back on the cot, she stared up at the beams in the ceiling and prayed for wisdom. *The pope isn't supposed to make mistakes*, she reminded herself. *But I have seen the hungry children hurt by his interdict. Our Lord said that God cares even for the sparrows, so he must want the pope to show mercy.* She rolled over and tried to rest.

The next morning, she spoke to Pope Gregory's secretary, asking for a meeting. He said he would see what he could do. But he never sent for her. So the next morning she asked again, and then the next morning. Finally, she was given a message. The pope would see her that evening.

An escort led her through a maze of carpeted corridors and into a brightly-lit hall. Jewel-studded crosses hung on every wall. Pope Gregory was slouched in his golden throne, his scepter on his lap. A young chamberlain knelt on the floor next to the throne. Behind them, like pillars against the wall, stood two armed guards at attention.

When he saw her, the pope straightened. "Come," he called.

She kneeled before him. The boy quickly brushed aside the golden fringe along the hem of the pope's robe and removed a red silk slipper, exposing a shriveled foot. She kissed it.

"Welcome to Avignon, Sister Catherine," said Pope Gregory. "Your reputation precedes you."

She gazed up at him. He smiled, the lines around his eyes creasing into his silver temples.

"Successor of Saint Peter, it is an honor to have your ear."

He motioned to her to rise. "You are welcome in my palace."

"It is a splendid palace," she said. "Your hospitality is gracious."

He struggled to raise himself in his throne. "I am not an old man, but you wouldn't know that by looking at me, would you? I'm afraid my constant illnesses have aged me before my time."

"I pray every day for your health, Holy Father."

"Bless you."

"There seem to be a good many guards around you. Are you in danger?"

Chuckling, he replied, "As long as the Florentine ambassadors are here, yes."

"I beg you not to worry about them. They have promised to be proper guests in your house."

He did not reply.

"Speaking of your residence, may I ask how long you plan to stay in Avignon?"

"What do you mean? This is where I live."

"Yes, but didn't you once promise to take the papacy back to Rome?"

He looked startled. "Of course, of course. All in good time, sister. But first I must deal with the Florentines."

"That's why I am here. I promised the Florentine chancellor I would present his case to you, with your permission."

He shifted. "I read your letters. They were very insightful."

"Father, can't the church help the Florentines? I have seen their desperate conditions first hand. Your mercy toward them would go far in promoting the gospel."

"Those desperate conditions are their own doing. Do you think I wanted that?" He shook his gray head. "But they continue to rebel against me and attack my army."

She took a deep breath. "Do you know that the flag they fly from the palace tower says *Liberty* on it? I have met with their Council of Eight. They only want freedom from tyrants."

"What tyrants?" Gregory exploded. "They've been under the church's protection for years!"

"Tyrants that pretend to be a part of this church!" she replied with blazing eyes. "The leaders you appointed stole the citizens' money and seized their property, and then withheld bread from them when they began to starve!"

He did not reply. She looked down at her hands, wondering if she had been too bold. But then he spoke.

"I could not have known about that."

My letters told you that! she thought. *And so did the chancellor's first ambassadors who were ignored.* Aloud, she said, "Of course not, Father. To suggest otherwise would cast improper suspicions on your holiness."

He glared at her, and again she dropped her eyes.

"Now that I'm aware of the problem," he said irritably, "I shall consider a solution. What do they propose?"

"They want you to remove the interdict against them, and release them from the church's control over their government," she said in a milder tone. "They will, of course, obey the church's authority in spiritual matters."

He raised an eyebrow. "Sister, you ought to know that ultimately *everything* is spiritual, even government. You have promoted the Crusades!"

"This is different."

"How?"

"The purpose of the Crusades is to take back from pagans what rightfully belongs to the church. But the Florentines are Christians who simply want peace."

He was quiet.

"I'm sure they will work out a compromise that will please you," she urged.

"Come back in the morning," he said finally. "You will be

my guest at a lovely breakfast, and then I will tell you my decision."

"Thank you, Father. I will glad to share your company again."

Raymond met her on her way to the cloister. "Success?" he wanted to know.

"We shall find out tomorrow," was the reply.

They were startled by sudden shouts down the corridor. Running toward the noise, they came upon two of the Florentine ambassadors pinned to the floor by guards.

"Remove your hands!" the ambassadors were shouting. "We will not be treated like this!"

"What is going on here?" Raymond demanded.

"We caught them trying to sneak into the pope's chambers with a dagger," explained one of the guards. "Please step aside. These men are dangerous."

Catherine glared at the ambassadors. "Is this true?"

"The dagger is to protect us against these goons!" said one of the ambassadors. "We were not threatening the pope. We just insisted that he grant us an audience."

"Why?" she demanded.

"We heard he was going to reject your peace proposal."

"Have you forgotten that Chancellor Salutati put this mission in my hands, not yours?"

"The chancellor gave us orders, too. If you failed, we were to negotiate."

"I have only just come from my meeting with the pope," she said sharply. "I have not failed yet, and I have a far better chance of succeeding than a couple of would-be assassins!"

She spun round and strode down the corridor as guards yanked the ambassadors to their feet. Raymond hurried after her. "You were right, Raymond," she said, her face flushed. "We shouldn't have trusted them."

"Do you think they really would have threatened the pope's life?"

She stopped walking. "I don't know."

"How will you explain this to Pope Gregory?"

"I will tell him the truth, that the people of Florence are desperate for better leadership."

"Are you saying the war is the pope's fault?"

Her serious face gave way to a smile. "You wouldn't answer when I asked that question!"

"Yes, but I am your confessor. You can tell me."

She shook her head. "This hallway isn't the confessional."

"So what options do we have now?"

"The same as before," said Catherine. "Tomorrow I will beg the pope to remove the interdict. Until then, we must double our prayers."

She spent the night on her knees in the women's cloister.

Dawn washed over Avignon in pink and purple strokes. Catherine left the cloister before the other women rose and walked to the palace. She needed a good stretch after her night on the cobblestones.

The sun was peeking above the towers by the time she was directed to one of the palace gardens to join the pope. A marble-topped table set with glistening pewter was nestled among the roses.

"Dominicans are not used to such finery," said Catherine after she had kissed the pope's hand. The array of cold meats, fruit, and pastries was a far cry from her usual day-old bread and water.

"Even Dominicans deserve a good breakfast once in awhile," replied the pope with a twinkle in his eyes. "I did promise you a lovely breakfast."

A butler offered her a pot of tea, but she waved him away. "Yes, about promises," she said.

"Right to business, eh?"

"Will you at least consider peace talks with the Florentines?"

"You mean the thugs who tried to break into my chambers last night? Your friends do not seem to share your desire for peace."

She set down the roll she was nibbling. "They were very wrong to do what they did. I have already written to the chancellor to set him straight. But, Father, you must understand that their people are dying! And because of it, the name of Christ is mocked. Surely you are concerned about that."

He stopped chewing. "You are a hard person to say no to, Catherine."

"Then you will remove the interdict?"

He shook his head. "It is a far more complicated situation than you know. I must give it more thought. But I promise I'll send someone there soon to look into matters more closely."

"That's not a very specific promise."

"It's the best I can do at this time."

"Very well. I will gladly tell them you are willing to consider negotiations." She held his gaze.

"There is something else?" he asked.

"With your permission, Father, I have another request, which surely you can perform."

He gave her a benevolent smile. "Anything."

"I mentioned it yesterday, and in one of my letters."

"Ah, yes," he said, selecting a second pastry from the butler's tray. "I assume you're talking about my returning to Rome."

She pushed aside her plate, the uneaten roll in the middle, and turned intense eyes on him. "Do that which you have promised," she said firmly.

"You must realize what a task it would be to move the entire Curia back to Rome," said Gregory. "We've been here for nearly seventy-five years."

"But Rome has been the center of the church for centuries. The Curia will go where you go. And you would be much closer to Florence and the other papal states, so you can keep a closer eye on the leaders who serve you there."

"And closer to the Anti-papal League!"

"But once you have demonstrated your desire for peace with the Florentines, they will no longer be a threat."

He did not look up.

"You promised that you would return the papacy to Rome someday. And you are ill. How many years do you have left on this earth to do it? What will happen to the people of Florence if the next pope decides to stay here, too?"

He set down his knife and stopped her with his hand. "If I let you keep talking, what else will you request?" He sighed. "You are right, I can see that. I will fulfill my promise and return the papacy to Rome."

"Thank you!" She rose.

"There is no need to hurry away, sister. You've hardly eaten, and after all the arguments you have made, you must certainly have worked up an appetite!"

"The Holy Father is too gracious," she said. "But I must not spoil myself or I will be tempted to leave the Dominicans!"

He laughed. "I admire your strength of character, sister. You are a godly woman. May God go with you."

She found Raymond in a nearby chapel.

"What did he say? You look satisfied."

She grimaced. "He is not ready to remove the interdict, but he will consider peace talks with Florence."

"That's a start! And?"

"And he promised to return the papacy to Rome."

"Two successes, Catherine! You are quite a negotiator."

She stared past him, going over the conversation in her head. "I can only hope that once he is back in Rome, he will reach out to the people of Italy and the famine will end."

"Centuries ago, the first Pope Gregory fought for the safety of the people of Rome," he reminded her. "This Gregory may yet live up to his name."

"I'll pray it is so. In the meantime, I want to return to Florence and do what I can to help the people."

"Perhaps this time you will go as the pope's ambassador to Florence, instead of the other way around!"

"If that is the role God has for me, I will gladly fulfill it."

She left him in the chapel and hurried back to the cloister to tell the sisters her news.

That September, Pope Gregory sailed back to Rome with the Curia. Shortly after, he appointed Catherine his ambassador to Florence in the interests of peace. He died within a year.

Catherine suffered a stroke and died on April 29, 1380, after founding several monasteries for women and writing The Dialogue, *a collection of essays on spiritual life.*

By the next century, Florence's prosperity had been restored and it became a leading city of the Renaissance.

John Wyclif: I will not die, but live and declare the works of the Lord

FEBRUARY 1377. LONDON, ENGLAND.

THE SETTING SUN cast a fiery glow on the surface of the Thames. Dozens of people hastened along the road south of London, most trying to get back to the city before curfew. Among the few going the other direction was a frail man with a long white beard. The cold air made his nose drip onto his whiskers, and he swiped at them with the tattered sleeve of his robe.

It had snowed briefly the day before, and now the ruts in the cobbled streets overflowed with muddy slush. Hobbling barefoot, he did his best to avoid the puddles, but the traffic was unkind. Carriage wheels rumbled behind him and he cringed even before the dark, icy spray rained down on him.

He wiped his face with his sleeve again, but it was too damp to do any good. With a low "woah!" from the driver, the horses pulled back and the carriage jerked to a stop a few paces ahead of him. The door swung open. "Doctor Wyclif!" cried a woman's voice.

He recognized the carriage then, and bent himself into a deep bow before the open door.

"Look at you! You're covered with mud! I am so sorry, doctor. My driver should have been more careful."

He raised his eyes. The most beautiful woman in all of England was leaning out the door, her lips curved into an apologetic smile.

"Princess Joan! It is always a pleasure to meet you, no matter the circumstances."

She laughed at him and reached out a gloved hand. "I assume you are on your way to Savoy Palace? Come, ride with me the rest of the way."

He let her pull him inside and tuck a heavy fur around him on the leather seat. The carriage lurched into motion again, rocking him against the satin draperies. It was much warmer in here than in the street.

"You must be a guest at the duke's dinner party!" she exclaimed. "I am so glad. A party in my honor will be much more interesting in the company of the illustrious Oxford doctor."

"You are too kind, princess," he insisted. "The honor is mine."

She leaned against the cushions and laughed again. Bundled into her furs, only her head was exposed, but it was clear why she was known throughout England as the Fair Maid of Kent. She had the complexion of a porcelain doll, a shapely nose, a pair of delicately arched brows. Her green eyes sparkled like the jewels in her gold circlet. Below the crown, her famous auburn hair was twisted into twin coils above her ears and covered with fine netting.

"I must say, however, that you do not look the role, Doctor Wyclif. A lecturer with no shoes must cause a stir at the university!"

He batted a hand at her teasing. "They're used to my non-traditional attire. A priest must live simply, I say. I would not trade the riches of Christ for all the riches of the world."

"So you are still causing trouble then?"

"If preaching the truth causes trouble, so be it!" But he smiled. "How is young Richard?"

"My son is healthy, thanks be to God. But he misses his father." A shadow flitted across her face. "It has been over six months now."

"All of England misses the Black Prince, my lady."

They paused at the huge iron gates of the Savoy and waited for the duke's guards to swing them aside. The driver clucked at the horses again and they pulled down the neat row of barren trees and into the circle drive, stopping before the massive wooden doors.

"Until dinner then," she said, as Wyclif helped her down to the waiting footmen.

She was whisked into the palace. The old man climbed down and followed with considerably less ceremony.

The corridors were full of clerks concluding the Duke of Lancaster's business for the day. They nodded at Wyclif. He was a friend of the duke's, and a frequent guest.

In the great hall, he paused before a portrait of the duke. It was framed in hand-carved moulding that had been rubbed with gold. The artist had captured the duke's intelligent eyes, long nose, and neatly-trimmed beard. His arms and legs displayed lustrous armor under a black and red tunic bearing his coat of arms, and he wore a gold crown. It was a good likeness.

He continued to the dining hall, pausing at the entrance while he was announced. The custom was too formal for him, but he had no intention of insulting his hosts.

"John Wyclif, priest of Lutterworth and Oxford doctor of theology," cried the herald.

He went in.

Red walls rose from the checkered floor to the gilded ceiling. Harp and lute players strummed quietly in a low balcony at the far end of the room. The coat of arms was repeated here, a large display in the center of the main wall.

It was a quartered royal shield. The upper right and lower left corners of the shield depicted three lions of England bearing their claws. The upper left and lower right corners contained the traditional *fleurs-de-lis* of France. It had been the proud shield of the duke's family since his father, King Edward III of England, had claimed the French throne forty years ago.

A number of guests had already arrived. They mingled in their bright clothes around a massive table, elegantly set for a crowd. Among the guests, he recognized Sir Henry Percy, the new marshal of England, and William Courtenay, London's popular young bishop.

A servant showed him to a seat near the center of the table.

"No." Wyclif shook his head. "I'm sure this is not my seat." He knew seating was based on rank, and with this guest list, he would likely be furthest from the host.

"This is the correct seat," insisted the servant. "The princess requested you sit next to her."

He waited uncomfortably behind his chair.

"Joan of Kent, Princess of Wales."

The Fair Maid swept in as she was announced, bestowing a welcoming smile on the whole room. She was still dressed in mourning for her husband, in a black gown with a wide neckline and a sweeping train. Her pointed sleeves, split at the elbows, draped nearly to the floor. She moved gracefully toward Wyclif and leaned in to whisper above the music.

"I hope you don't mind entertaining me," she said. "I asked for you to be seated next to me."

"It is very kind of you, as usual, but I'm afraid the other guests are less pleased with the arrangement."

"You mean Courtenay?" She eyed the bishop, who was frowning in their direction. "He'll get over it."

The musicians fell silent then as the hosts entered the doorway.

"John of Gaunt, King of Castile and Leon, Duke of Lancaster,

Duke of Burgundy, Earl of Lincoln and Leicester, Lord of Beaufort and Nogent, of Bergerac, et cetera, et cetera. His wife, the Duchess of Lancaster, Constance of Castile."

The couple entered to the applause of their guests. Everyone waited until Duke John seated the duchess on his left, seated the princess on his right, and then took his own place at the center of the table. Then they scrambled for their seats. Wyclif lowered himself uncomfortably on the edge of his chair next to the princess.

"Welcome!" the duke said, spreading his hands across the table. He wore a white fur collar over a blue velvet jacket and looked every part the royal English host. "Thank you all for gracing my table tonight." He turned to Joan. "It is a special honor to welcome you, fair princess. Your presence distinguishes this gathering like a rare jewel."

"Don't be so formal with your sister-in-law!" She laughed and raised her goblet. "To a delicious dinner and fascinating conversation!"

"Hear, hear!"

Duke John waved at the musicians to take up their instruments again, and the butlers begin to flit in and out with the first course.

Wyclif slurped his soup quietly, listening as the guests struck up clusters of conversation. A lady at the end of the table praised Bishop Courtenay's last sermon. Someone commented on how delightfully the musicians played. The princess and Sir Percy laughed at a story the duchess told.

Duchess Constance turned to him then. "Doctor Wyclif, how delightful that you could join us," she said, her eyes wandering to the mud stains on his brown robe.

"Please pardon my appearance," he said. "I preached in three churches today, and I'm afraid the streets are a bit messy this winter."

"I hear you have been working hard for the duke these last few months in London."

"I've been working hard for the cause of the gospel," he said, softening the rebuke with a smile.

The duke winked at his wife. "The truth is that I am working hard for Doctor Wyclif, rather than the other way around. It is my duty to support forward-thinkers like him."

The princess chuckled at his elbow. "Especially if his forward-thinking keeps more silver in the coffers of England."

"That is just a side benefit," said Sir Percy, hiding his grin behind his sleeve as he wiped his mouth.

"It is perfectly reasonable that church reform would have a positive impact on the government of England," Wyclif said, reaching for the salt cellar. "But that is not my purpose. My purpose is to correct the abuses of the church."

"What abuses?"

The buzz of conversation died away.

"The church can't be guilty of abuses," said Bishop Courtenay emphatically. "She is the bride of Christ!"

"She is no longer the pure bride she once was," replied Wyclif.

Courtenay put his elbows on the table and leaned in. "That is a dangerous accusation, doctor. Tell me, how has the church sullied her reputation?"

Wyclif felt all eyes on him. Even the musicians had stopped playing and were peering over the balcony.

"God has blessed his church with great wealth," he said. "There are a hundred churches in London alone, nearly one on every street! Instead of distributing this wealth to the poor, the bishops spend it on bigger cathedrals."

"It is proper to decorate God's house. The Jews melted their gold earrings to build the tabernacle according to God's instructions."

"True," admitted Wyclif. "But Jesus said that a cup of cold

water given to the thirsty was an act of mercy befitting his gospel. Instead, our church pads her pockets when the poor don't even have pockets!"

"Jesus also said the poor would always be with us."

"He didn't mean not to help them!"

"The pope demands taxes from the king," broke in Duke John. "But England belongs to Christ, not to the pope. If the church of England cares for her own needs, what does she owe the pope?"

"The paying of tithes is a spiritual duty," declared the bishop.

Wyclif shook his head. "The less the church is concerned with wealth and power, the more she can fulfill her spiritual duties. And how can she fulfill those duties when her bishops commit sins of gluttony and pride?"

Now Courtenay was on his feet. "Are you accusing me of those sins?"

"No," said Wyclif sincerely. "All of London knows you are a godly man, and no one can rightly accuse you of such things. But that is not true of every bishop. And there are many other things we must change, too. We hold our services in Latin. How can the unlearned know anything about their faith when they don't speak Latin? We tell them to love God's word, but we keep it out of the English language. Why can the French have a translation, but the English cannot?"

"If we translate the Scriptures into English, every fool will believe himself a bishop! What heresies will we have on our hands if the Bible is in theirs?"

"We must work harder to teach correct doctrine then."

"You are unwise to speak so poorly of the church of God."

The duchess waved flustered hands. "I beg your pardon, gentlemen. I'm afraid I started this discussion with my innocent questions. You'll forgive me? I do hope we can finish our dinner in peace."

"No, you'll forgive me, duchess," said the bishop, retaking his seat with a regal nod. "I did not mean to take advantage of your hospitality. The good doctor and I will have this conversation another time."

"Yes, today is dedicated to the flower of England!" said the duke, raising his glass toward the princess.

"Yes, we seem to have forgotten about me," said Joan with another laugh. "Where is the next course of this delicious meal? I may have to steal your cooks, Constance!"

The guests relaxed and a pleasant murmur of conversation stirred again. The musicians returned to their instruments. Wyclif accepted a piece of broiled fish from a butler and ate hungrily. Bishop Courtenay glared at him for the rest of the evening.

As the guests were leaving, the princess pulled Wyclif aside. "You are brave to take on the bishop—or the pope, I suppose. You must know they will make trouble for you."

"I am simply speaking the truth," he said. "It is unpleasant, but it must be said."

"Yes, but be careful. The bishop knows full well what you've been preaching in his city. He's looking for evidence to bring you to trial."

The duke appeared at her side. "Courtenay believes you are simply my tool for getting the government more power over the church," he said to Wyclif.

The doctor shrugged. "If the church won't perform her duties to the people, then it is up to the government to help the people, even if that means taking back the church's funds and property."

"I agree," said Duke John. "That is why I have supported you for the last five months. It is not in my best interests to discourage your work. But your position grows more dangerous every day."

"We must pray harder for our reforms. The truth will not be silenced on my watch."

His companions were quiet. Then the princess broke into a smile. "Thank you for the entertaining battle with the bishop," she said. "Now I must pay my respects to our hostess. Good night, doctor. Good night, John." She swept toward the duchess at the door.

"It's late, beyond London's curfew," said the duke, "and you are looking rather tired. You may as well spend the night here. I have a meeting in the city in the morning, and you can ride in with me."

"Very well. I wasn't looking forward to the walk anyway. I'm not as young as I used to be."

The duke laughed. "Who is, doctor?"

The two of them were in the duke's private office at the Savoy a week later when a message arrived for Wyclif.

"It's a summons from Courtenay," said the doctor. "He and the Archbishop of Canterbury have called me to stand trial at Saint Paul's Cathedral and explain my beliefs."

"Explain your beliefs? Compared to you, the bishops are practically illiterate!" declared the duke.

"Courtenay and Archbishop Sudbury are reasonable men. I'm sure we can have a civil discussion."

"Even so, I suggest we get a few friars to help you with your defense. And it would be a good idea to take the marshal along with us, in case the bishop decides to take action."

Word of the summons spread through the city as fast as the plague.

On the day of the trial, Duke John accompanied Wyclif to the cathedral. Sir Percy and some of his men went with them. They were surprised to find nearly the whole city waiting for them.

"This can't be for me!" said Wyclif.

"I'm afraid it's my fault," said Percy, keeping his hand on the hilt of his sword. "The people find me a bit heavy-handed with the law. They're here to protest my involvement in church matters."

The cathedral was the tallest building in London and a center for legal transactions. Today there were so many people in the courtyard, some had even climbed up to Saint Paul's Cross, a platform with a giant stone cross where public announcements were often made. Percy's men had to threaten and shove to clear a path into the church and through the long nave to the chapel at the other end.

Bishop Courtenay and Archbishop Sudbury were waiting for them at the altar.

"If I had known you were bringing an army with you, Lord Percy, I'd have seen to it that you were not invited," declared Courtenay.

As many people who could fit had followed them into the chapel. They hooted at the bishop's sharp words.

"This is a public building, Courtenay," said the duke. "Percy has as much right to be here as you do."

Percy glared at the bishop and put a firm hand on Wyclif's slight shoulder. "It took a bit of an effort to get in here, didn't it, doctor? I think you should sit down and rest yourself. You don't look well."

That launched a new wave of clamor. *Nobody* was allowed to sit during a trial.

"You will remain standing, doctor," demanded Courtenay. "It is Percy's fault you had such a hard time getting here, not mine."

"Percy's motion is reasonable," Duke John insisted. "And I've had enough of your arrogance, Lord Bishop. If I must, I will bring down all the prideful bishops in England!"

"Do your worst, sir!"

The crowd pressed forward. The trial had not yet begun and already it was more entertaining than they had hoped.

"You think you cannot be touched because you are a wealthy bishop?" Duke John had his hands on his hips.

"My confidence is in nothing but God, with whose assistance I will be bold enough to examine this wayward priest!"

The duke turned to Percy. "Perhaps it is time to pluck this bishop from the church like a hair is plucked from a head!"

The crowd rushed at them. "Keep your hands off our bishop!" they shouted.

"That's enough!" cried Archbishop Sudbury. "This is a church. You are in the presence of God! Come to order!"

But Courtenay and Sudbury could no longer see Wyclif or his protectors. In the chaos, the trio had slipped out of the cathedral and returned to Savoy Palace.

When the crowd realized they were gone, they went home. Percy was right. They hadn't come to see what would befall the frail priest, but to object to the new marshal.

Wyclif returned to his teaching at Oxford. Every day in the quiet refectory, he sat in a hard-backed wooden chair facing a row of students. Beside him, a large copy of whatever text they were studying was propped on a stand so all could see. He lectured for the first hour, then prodded the students to ask and answer questions on the subject. There were several classes a day, scheduled between meals and prayer services.

One of his students, John Aston, was so moved by Wyclif's teaching that he insisted on dressing like the doctor. Aston and a fellow student named Nicholas Hereford began helping Wyclif translate the Bible into English. Every day they took the few pages they completed to the scriptorium, where other students copied them and bound the new pages with the previous ones to be distributed in the bookshops of Oxford.

Three significant announcements reached Wyclif at the university that year.

In the spring, he learned that Pope Gregory had left Avignon in September and returned the papacy to Rome. Critics had been calling for the return to Rome for years, but it wasn't until the

Dominican sister Catherine of Sienna urged him that Gregory finally agreed. It had taken months for the word to reach England. *Perhaps the move demonstrates that the pope is open to reform*, wondered Wyclif.

In June, King Edward III died. England mourned. John of Gaunt was appointed guardian of Prince Richard, Joan's 11-year-old son. Richard was now king, and the duke was busy handling his affairs.

In December, Wyclif's friend Alan Tonworth, chancellor of Oxford, brought him a disturbing letter. Wyclif was in the refectory with Aston and Hereford discussing the place of science in theology.

"Apparently you have enemies in high places," said Chancellor Tonworth, waving the letter. "Someone sent a list of accusations against you to Rome, and the pope is furious. He is calling for your imprisonment and trial."

"The pope has no such authority to arrest an Englishman!" cried Hereford. "Only the government can put someone in prison."

"He's ordered it anyway," said Chancellor Tonworth. "The pope believes he rules the world."

"This is the very abuse of power I've been writing and preaching about," said Wyclif, scowling. "He takes farmland from the poor to build a new cathedral. When the citizens resist, like in Florence, he just sends his mercenaries in to murder them and take it anyway!"

Aston began to pace up and down the long hall. "What are you going to do, chancellor?"

"The pope is threatening to take over Oxford if we don't examine him for heresy," said Tonworth.

"Then examine me," Wyclif insisted. "Oxford is capable of identifying truth or heresy without the pope's threats! Gather all the doctors and I will explain my views."

The examination took place within days. His answers satisfied the other lecturers, but they were hesitant to pick a fight with the pope. "Perhaps until we sort this out with Rome, you will stay in Black Hall?" one of them suggested. "We can assure the pope we have complied with his arrest order, and you will be a lot more comfortable here than in the Tower of London!"

Wyclif agreed, for their sake. But the solution did not satisfy the bishops of England. Alan Tonworth was fired as chancellor of Oxford. Wyclif was ordered to appear in March at a new trial at Lambeth Palace, Archbishop Sudbury's castle.

From Oxford, he was escorted to the Thames to board the archbishop's barge, and then across to the south bank. The castle towers cast long, rippling shadows on the surface of the river. The mist was cold, and Wyclif shivered, tucking his bare feet under the hem of his robe.

Sudbury had a roomy chapel on the second floor of one of the towers. He was waiting, with Bishop Courtenay and a number of other English bishops, when Wyclif was led upstairs.

"Well, Doctor Wyclif, it's time we got back to this trial," Sudbury declared. His colleagues stood on either side of him, resplendent in their embroidered robes and pointed miters.

"John of Gaunt and Henry Percy will not be present today," Courtenay added. "This time there will be no threats or riots to distract us from the pursuit of justice."

"I am prepared to defend my teachings," replied Wyclif, facing the bishops. "I preach only what I sincerely believe is the Word of God. If you show me where I am wrong, I will repent of my errors and submit to the church."

Courtenay shrugged. "Then this trial need not be long."

A list of charges was read.

"What do you have to say for yourself?" asked the archbishop.

Wyclif stood tall, though his tired legs were trembling. "Some of these accusations are true. I do believe no one can be excommunicated by the church who has not first severed himself from God by his sins. I do believe that the state can and must refuse to pay tithes to corrupt bishops. But—!" He jabbed at the air with his index finger. "Many of your accusations are unfounded. You have misunderstood my teachings."

"Enlighten us!"

"I speak the truth when I say that the devil himself reigns among the clergy! They crave power and wealth and will do whatever they can to keep from being exposed."

"Words like that will not deliver you from punishment!" thundered Sudbury.

There was a sudden commotion in the hall outside. A guard slipped in with a whispered message for the archbishop. Sudbury frowned.

"The council welcomes Sir Lewis Clifford," he said in a voice that did not sound at all welcoming.

Wyclif raised a curious eyebrow and turned to the door with the bishops. He had heard of Clifford. He was a distant relative of Princess Joan and had fought in battle with John of Gaunt. The knight marched in, but he was not alone. A crowd of noisy Londoners followed him. At the front were Aston and Hereford. Aston winked at his lecturer.

"Quiet!" Archbishop Sudbury demanded.

Sir Clifford stopped a few paces from the archbishop and made a graceful bow. When he drew himself back to his full height, his voice rang through the now-packed chapel. "I come as an emissary of Joan of Kent, princess of Wales, to deliver a message to Archbishop Sudbury."

Sudbury was still frowning. "State your message, knight. You know who I am."

"The princess has received the pope's letter asking for her support in the matter of Doctor Wyclif. The church may pass judgment on Doctor Wyclif as you see fit, she says, but the government will not carry out your sentences. Excommunicate him if you will, but there will be no torture or execution of heretics in England!"

The crowd broke into shouts and applause.

Courtenay pulled the archbishop aside. "This is a familiar situation," he warned.

"Too familiar!" nodded Sudbury.

"We must act quickly. We are about to lose this opportunity as we did the first."

"But this time these fickle people care what happens to the priest. I will not have a riot in my own home, Courtenay."

The archbishop raised his hands to silence the people. "Quiet! Quiet!" He adjusted his robes and faced them calmly. "No one will be tortured or executed," he reassured the crowd. "However, this council forbids Doctor Wyclif to preach on any of the matters about which he has been examined today."

The people stamped and cheered. Sudbury pushed Courtenay out a side exit. Sir Clifford took the frail doctor by the elbow and hurried him out to the barge.

A distinctive carriage was waiting at the dock on the other side of the river. Clifford hoisted the doctor inside and shut the door firmly.

It took a moment for his eyes to adjust to the dim interior. John of Gaunt and Princess Joan were smiling at him from the facing bench.

"So you *were* behind this!" Wyclif said to the duke.

"No, it was Joan," he insisted. "She told me about the pope's letter and urged me to intervene."

She leaned forward in a rustle of silk and patted Wyclif's knee. "I didn't want you to lose your head, doctor."

He bowed as best he could in the seat. "You are too gracious, princess. Perhaps we should call you the Fair *and Benevolent* Maid of Kent!"

"Your life is safe for now, but the council has forbidden you to teach," said the duke. "What will you do?"

"I'll ignore them!" cried Wyclif. "It is like the Prophet Jeremiah said. The truth is a fire shut up in my bones!"

"Well, we'll try to protect you, prophet, but perhaps you should stop referring to the pope as the antichrist!" Joan's eyes twinkled.

"Let Courtenay and the others do what they may," retorted Wyclif. "If I can't teach at Oxford, I'll find a street corner where I can preach. And I'll continue to help my former students with their English translation of the Bible." He shut his eyes and propped his bare feet against the cushions. "With the Psalmist, I say, 'I will not die, but live and declare the works of the Lord.'"

"Yes, but first," said the duke, wrinkling his nose, "let's get you a bath and a pair of shoes. Even a humble priest should have *one* pair, Wyclif!" He stuck his head out the door. "To the Savoy, driver."

The carriage lurched into motion, and they pulled away from the dock with a muddy splash.

Pope Gregory died a few days after Wyclif's trial, but it was several months before word arrived in England, and even longer before they heard that two rival popes were fighting to take his place.

William Courtenay became Archbishop of Canterbury.

John Wyclif continued to write against the abuses of the church, with the protection of the Duke of Lancaster. The frail doctor's health declined, and he died from a second stroke on December 28, 1384. But the Bible translation he supervised circulated throughout England, and his call for reform spread across Europe. At the Council of Constance, long after his death, the church officially declared him a heretic. They dug up his body and burned it, scattering his ashes into a river.

Councils of the Medieval Church

MEDIEVAL CHURCH COUNCILS were arranged to correct heresy and decide matters of church business. In the Middle Ages, many decisions made at these councils introduced new teachings. Later, during the Protestant Reformation, those teachings were challenged as unbiblical.

The first seven ecumenical councils are considered the most important by Catholics, Eastern Orthodox, and Protestants. The first four councils were called by the early church: the Council of Nicea in 325, the First Council of Constantinople in 381, the Council of Ephesus in 432, and the Council of Chalcedon in 451. Three more were held during the medieval period:

THE SECOND COUNCIL OF CONSTANTINOPLE (553)

This is also called the Fifth Ecumenical Council. There were 164 bishops present. It was called by Pope Vigilius (died in 555) and Emperor Justinian I (483-565). This council condemned a teaching which incorrectly understood the divine and human natures of Christ, and confirmed the declarations made a hundred years earlier by the Council of Chalcedon.

THE THIRD COUNCIL OF CONSTANTINOPLE (680)

This was also called the Sixth Ecumenical Council, was held by Pope Agatho (died in 681) and led by Emperor Constantine Pogonatus (649-685). One hundred seventy-four bishops came, plus the patriarchs of Constantinople and Antioch. This council condemned another false teaching about Jesus and excommunicated those who held to it.

THE SECOND COUNCIL OF NICEA (787)

This council is also known as the Seventh Ecumenical Council. Their concern was the *Iconoclastic Controversy*. In 726, Byzantine Emperor Leo III (717-741) had prohibited the use of *icons* (or images of Christ, angels, Mary, and the saints) in worship. The eastern church continued to use icons in worship, while the western church called it idolatry. Three hundred and fifty bishops came to this council to affirm the value of icons, but condemned their use in worship.

OTHER MEDIEVAL COUNCILS

Other councils were held in the medieval period, usually in response to another heresy, and sometimes to call a Crusade. Most of the decisions made during these councils are rejected by Protestants. The First Lateran Council (1123) forbade priests, deacons, and monks from marrying. The members of the Fourth Lateran Council (1215) confirmed the teaching that during communion, the bread and wine turn into the actual body and blood of Christ (one of the most rejected teachings during the Reformation). It was during the Council of Constance (1414-1418) that John Wyclif (1329-1384) and John Hus (1369-1415), were condemned. Both these men called for reform in the church.

John Hus: This Goose is Not Afraid of Being Cooked

APRIL 1414. A ROAD SOUTH OF PRAGUE, IN BOHEMIA.

TWO HORSES PICKED their way along the washed-out road. "Praise be to God. The rain has finally stopped," exclaimed one of the riders. "It's been a month since I saw the sun!" He raised his face gratefully to the warm rays.

His companion scowled. "Yes, but now the mud is just baking into our armor. I may never get these clean again!" He scraped at the thick crust covering his breeches.

"Forget about the mud. We're here. Look—there it is, around this stand of trees."

They reigned in their horses at the edge of the moat and peered across. On the far side of the water, the outer wall of a castle rose from the banks. A green smear of algae coated the stones at the waterline. The iron gate was down, locked in place in front of the massive wooden doors. The castle appeared lifeless. But the knights were not easily fooled.

"Hail, lord of the castle!" the second knight called.

The only response from across the moat was a scraping sound as a tiny window in the gate slid open. "Where is your lord's hospitality?" shouted the knight again.

After a pause, a muffled voice came through the opening. "Who goes there?"

"Lord John of Chlum, and my comrade, Lord Wenceslas of Dubá. We are knights of King Sigismund."

"What is your business?"

"We've come for the fugitive."

There was a pause. Then, "You have the wrong castle."

"Right," muttered Lord Wenceslas.

"We know you're protecting the priest," yelled Lord John. "We've come to ensure he is safely transported to Constance as ordered."

The wall was silent.

Wenceslas raised himself in his saddle. "It is not in your best interests to cross Sigismund!"

The window scraped shut. After a pause, chains groaned as the wooden bridge was lowered over the moat and the gate was raised into the wall.

"That's better!" Wenceslas mumbled.

Urging their horses forward, the knights clattered across the bridge. They halted just inside a small courtyard where a dozen people were waiting for them. From his perch in an empty wagon, a scrawny dog growled at them and bared his teeth.

A tall man stepped forward. "I am Lord Ctibor of Kozí and this is my castle. You have requested my hospitality as men of honor, and I will give it."

"Then you are also a man of honor," said Lord John. "Where may we find John Hus?"

"Where he always is. In the tower writing."

The knight swung down from his horse. "Show Lord Wenceslas

to your stable and take me to the priest."

Ctibor sent a boy with Wenceslas and led Lord John through a heavy arch to a circular staircase in the wall. The knight counted thirty-four narrow steps carved in the stone before he reached the cramped room at the top.

A single window lit the chamber. In the dim light, a cloaked figure leaned over a crude table, scratching furiously with his pen. Under his boxy rimmed cap, the man's nose angled sharply away from his face like an arrowhead. A bony chin was not disguised by the thin beard. Lord John recognized his profile before the priest turned toward his visitor.

"John Hus." The knight bowed. "I am Lord John of Chlum. I bring you letters from Sigismund, King of Hungary and Holy Roman Emperor."

The priest's dark eyes bored into him. "What does Sigismund want with me? Is he doing the church's business now?"

The knight held his gaze. "He is still waiting to be crowned, even though he was elected emperor three years ago. In the meantime, he wishes to reunite the church. But certain unresolved issues stand in the way."

"Issues like me, you mean."

"Your writings have ignited a fire throughout Bohemia and Hungary. The word *reform* is on nearly everyone's lips."

Hus spread his hands. "Ah, but everyone has a different definition. There are dozens of ideas about how the church needs to change, and no one seems to be listening to any of them."

"Some claim you are spreading the heresy of John Wyclif, the Oxford doctor."

"Then some are lying!"

"Do you not agree with Wyclif's teachings?"

"Only some of them," replied the priest. "But the heresies I have been accused of don't resemble my beliefs at all."

Ctibor had remained at the top of stairs, but now joined the conversation. "Perhaps if you didn't preach that the pope is corrupt, there would be no accusations against you at all!" he said with a wink.

"The king wants to clear up those charges in a fair, open discussion," explained Lord John. "He and the pope are calling a council at Constance and request your presence there."

"Which pope?" replied Hus. "There are three of them now! You see why I call for reform?"

Lord John shook his head. "Pope John XXIII is the true pope. The others are imposters."

"Says you."

"Says King Sigismund."

Hus slammed his fist down on the table. "Pope John is corrupt and power hungry! He preys on the fears of the people, selling them relics of the saints in exchange for eternal life. He kills anyone that agrees with John Wyclif's writings and burns any book that challenges his authority. Who gave him the right to do that?"

"He is the head of the church!"

A boy stepped out from the shadows at the top of the stairs. "Christ is the head of the church, not the pope," he said boldly.

"So you are making disciples while you hide in this tower," said Lord John.

"Peter of Mladonovice is my student and scribe," said Hus. "Join us, Peter. We are discussing my approaching trial and death."

"Don't be dramatic, Master Hus," chided the knight. "Lord Wenceslas and I have vowed to protect you with our lives. You will be given safe passage to Constance."

"I do not doubt your loyalty or Sigismund's word," replied Hus. "But you must forgive me if I laugh at the idea that the pope's word means anything. The archbishop of Prague has already excommunicated me, so I willingly left the city. What more does he want?"

The knight glanced away. "The pope is threatening to call a Crusade against Prague unless you back down."

"Against Prague?" cried Peter. "It's not a Muslim city!"

"The popes have forgotten why they called the Crusades in the first place," said the priest quietly. "All I want is justice. If I am wrong, let them show me from Scripture."

"You're a tough goose," declared Peter.

Lord John laughed. "Goose?"

"That's what the name *Hus* means. He's from the hamlet of Husinec, where they raise flocks of geese."

The priest rose regally. "This goose is not afraid of being cooked!"

"No one is going to be cooked," insisted Lord John. "This is just a misunderstanding that you can clear up in person at the council. Wenceslas and I will provide safe passage."

"I have a bad feeling about this council, but I welcome an honest debate." Hus drew his papers together. "Peter, gather our things. We'll give this good knight the opportunity to do his job."

They arrived in Constance a week after Pope John. The pope's gilded carriage had been escorted into the city by 600 attendants and scarlet-clad cardinals on white steeds. The city was still buzzing with excitement when Hus and Peter clattered through the town square in their horse-drawn wagon. Lord John was a few paces ahead, with Lord Wenceslas following at the rear.

A widow offered them rooms in her house on Saint Paul's Street. Hus had no money, but Lord John insisted on covering their expenses.

"I must report our arrival to the pope immediately," said the knight. "Wenceslas will remain here with you until I get back." He left them carrying their small bundles into the house.

The pope had taken up residence at a monastery on the outskirts of Constance. In the few days he had been there, he had turned it into more of a palace than a monastery. Lord John was escorted into his throne room by the pope's personal guards. Pope John was meeting with several cardinals. The knight immediately dropped to one knee and waited for permission to speak.

"Lord John of Chlum, I presume."

"Yes, Holy Father. I am loyal to King Sigismund of Hungary, as he is loyal to the church."

"You are the knight responsible for the heretic's protection?"

"Yes."

Pope John waved a ringed hand at the man next to him. "You know Cardinal Zabarella of Florence?"

Chlum nodded to the cardinal but kept his eyes on the pope. "I'm here to inform you that John Hus has arrived in Constance. Sigismund granted him safe passage in my custody. I assume he has your protection as well?"

The room grew suddenly quiet.

"Of course he is safe!" said the pope with annoyance. "Now, I must get back to the Lord's work. Your service to the church has been noted." He shifted back to the cardinal.

But Lord John wasn't finished. "Just so I understand, Holy Father," he insisted. "You give your word that no harm will come to Master Hus, even if the council excommunicates him as a heretic?"

Pope John swung around with a red face. "You insult me!" he cried. "I would injure no one, even if he had murdered my own brother! Now go!"

A guard appeared at Lord John's elbow, but the knight shook him off and marched out the door.

"That one must learn to be more respectful," declared the pope.

"Indeed." Cardinal Zabarella stared after him with a frown.

A week later, the priest was hunched over a book in the corner of his room when Lord John came looking for him. A spicy aroma drifted in from the firepit outside.

"Are you hungry, Master Hus?" asked the knight.

"Yes, I'm hungry for my freedom!"

"Will you settle for some stew? Apparently the widow's cooking is famous around here. Peter and Wenceslas will be back any minute now."

They sat at a table in the central room of the house. The old woman had been watching for them, and now set out steaming bowls and a wooden platter piled with dark bread. They had taken only a few bites when a *rap! rap! rap!* sounded at the door. Lord John crossed the small room in two steps and threw open the door.

A short man with wide red whiskers stood on the stoop. "I'm Dr. Ottobono," said the visitor through his mustache. "I'm the burgomaster of Constance."

"State your business," demanded the knight.

"I'm here with a few bishops. We came to request that Master Hus join us tonight. Some of the cardinals wish to interview him."

Hus stood up from the table and squared his shoulders. "I've agreed to meet with the whole council, not a few representatives."

"They just want to meet with you privately before the council begins. Won't you consider it, in the interests of peace?"

Lord John's eyes narrowed. He faced the visitor, feet slightly apart. "Will you uphold the pope's promise of safe conduct?"

"Of course!"

Hus glanced at his protector. "For the sake of peace, I will go with them for the evening," he agreed.

"Then I shall accompany you."

They tossed their cloaks around their shoulders and left their bowls on the table. But the moment they stepped out into the cool evening air, they were surrounded by armed soldiers.

"What is this?" cried Lord John, drawing his sword. "You promised safe passage!"

"Put your sword away!" insisted the burgomaster.

The knight ignored him. "Another step closer to Master Hus and some of you will not make it home tonight!"

The soldiers tightened the circle around them.

Hus glared at Dr. Ottobono accusingly. "This is how you work for peace?"

"Please, good knight," said the burgomaster, raising a fleshly hand in protest. "These soldiers are just here to ensure Master Hus' safe passage."

The priest took his protector by the elbow. "It is all right, my friend," he said. "I do not wish to see blood shed over a misunderstanding."

Lord John hesitated. *No one is better skilled with the sword than I, but there are too many of them.* "Very well," he said finally. He sheathed his blade, but kept a hand on the hilt. "Widow Fida!"

The old woman peeked out the door. "Yes, Lord John?"

"When Lord Wenceslas and the boy Peter arrive, let them know what has happened."

She nodded vigorously and dabbed at her eyes. "Good bye, Master Hus."

"Don't cry, my good woman," the priest said, waving her back into the house. "I'll be back to finish that delicious stew in a few hours."

"If you're not *in* the stew," muttered Lord John under his breath. "It looks to me like someone is preparing to roast a goose!"

They were taken to a large home at the center of the city. Lord John was not surprised when they were greeted by Cardinal Zabarella.

"Ah! My guests have arrived," the cardinal said, spreading his hands.

"Do you always send armed guards for your guests?" retorted Hus.

The cardinal's eyes glittered in the dim light. "Only when they are heretics." He turned to the soldiers. "Take Master Hus inside. The lord knight can wait for him out here."

They disappeared through the gate, leaving a man to guard the entrance. Lord John searched the perimeter of the house. Light spilled out from one of the arched windows on the east side. It was too high to see in, but he soon heard voices. Cardinal Zabarella was interrogating Hus. "Are you a follow of Wyclif?" he demanded.

"I am a follower of Christ!" insisted the priest.

There was a rustle of books. "These are Wyclif's forty-five articles. Read them and admit if you agree!"

The response was immediate and confident. "I know what Wyclif taught and I do not fully agree with at least thirty-three of these statements. You have misunderstood my writings if you believe I teach the same thing he did."

"That is not so!" broke in a third voice. Lord John did not recognize it. "Wyclif denied the teaching that the bread of communion is transformed into the actual body of Christ. Do you not agree with him?"

"I already answered the question. You are making up false accusations against me."

"That's a lie!"

A muffled cry was followed by crashes and scraping. Lord John dashed back to the gate. The doors of the house flung open, the soldiers pushing Hus ahead of them with his arms pinned to his sides.

"Where are you taking him?"

Two soldiers turned back. He swung a fist at one of them, knocking the soldier against the wall. Instantly, the other drew his sword, stopping it an inch from the knight's throat.

"Get out of here or you'll join the heretic in his prison cell," he snarled.

"King Sigismund promised this man safe conduct. You are in violation of that order."

The soldier bared his teeth in an unpleasant grin. "Your king has gone back on his promise."

"I have pledged my life to Sigismund! He would not do such a thing."

Cardinal Zabarella stepped out of the house and leered over the knight and his captors. "I'm afraid this thug is right," he laughed. "Giving up this heretic is a small price for Sigismund to pay if he wants to regain peace in his kingdom and receive his crown."

"Hus denied your accusations!" shouted the knight. "I heard him."

The cardinal shrugged. "He's lying, of course. That is what heretics do. Others have proven from his own writings that he is a heretic." He leaned closer, his breath hot on Lord John's face. "Now get out of here before I persuade your king to turn you in as well!"

The guards shoved him outside the gate. It was much darker now than when they had first arrived, and he could see only the flickering pools of torchlight in the street. He ran along the wall where they had dragged Hus away, but he heard nothing except his own footsteps on the cobblestones.

This is all wrong! he told himself. *Master Hus is a good man, and I vowed to protect him. There is only one thing to do.*

He dashed away toward the pope's monastery-turned-palace.

Pope John was in quiet conversation with a bishop when the clang of metal outside his room made him jump to his feet. The doors burst open as John of Chlum charged in.

"You are a liar!" he cried, brandishing his sword.

"Guards!" cried the pope.

"Your guards are not available right now," said Lord John, pointing to the knights sprawled on the floor outside. "What have you done with Master Hus?"

The pope raised both hands in protest. "I am not involved in this."

"Then free him immediately!" demanded Chlum, moving in closer.

Behind him, Cardinal Zabarella came through the doors. "This man leaves a trail of battered guards," he said, kicking one of the fallen swords out of his path. He took his place beside the pope. "I will explain everything, Holy Father. But for your own protection, you must lock this man up."

The cardinal's guards filed in behind him. Lord John snarled at them.

"Lord knight, put your sword away," insisted the pope. "I will not arrest you if you respect this office!"

"There is no one here for me to respect," he declared, and strode angrily out the door.

On his way back to Saint Paul's Street, he met Peter and Wenceslas.

"Widow Fida told us what happened," said Peter. "We have tracked them to a Dominican monastery."

"What are we waiting for? Let's go rescue him!"

Wenceslas put a hand on his comrade's arm. "There are dozens of guards. The three of us will never get past them."

Chlum stomped on a broken rock in the road.

"What's going on? He was already here for the council," said Wenceslas. "Why did they arrest him?"

"Sigismund has betrayed him, and us. Come on, we have to find another way to help Master Hus."

They spent weeks trying to get into the monastery with food and letters for the captive. But the guards turned them away every time.

The pope continued to deny it, but Lord John knew he was behind the priest's arrest. The knight visited every cardinal and bishop in the region, demanding that they support his friend. He threatened Dr. Ottobono. With Peter's help, he made posters arguing that Hus was being held illegally. Wenceslas nailed the announcements to the cathedral door for the people to read.

Some of the bishops began to speak out against the pope.

And then one morning, Pope John was gone.

"How did he escape?" bellowed Lord John when Peter brought him the news. "There are church officials all over this city!"

"They say he disguised himself as a workman and fled the city secretly under armed guard."

The knight paced, running a hand through his long curls. "How could I let him get away?"

"No, this is a blessing, John!" insisted Wenceslas. "If he is in hiding, he can no longer hurt Master Hus. And there is more! King Sigismund is on his way to Constance."

"It's about time! Maybe now we can get this trial over with." He ran for the door. "I'll be back."

Hus had been given paper and ink in his cell. It was hard to make use of it with one hand shackled to the wall, but there was nothing else to do. He spent most of his time hunched over the papers spread on the floor, one arm chained above him.

If I can only get my day in front of the council, then I can convince them I'm not a heretic! I just want the chance to explain my ideas about reform. He was dragging his one free hand across the page, smearing the ink, when he heard footsteps on the staircase.

A guard eased open the door. "We have a new prisoner at the castle," he said casually.

Hus stared at him.

"He's even more well known than you."

"You came up here to tell me that?"

"I thought you might be interested."

"Why? Who is he?"

The guard sneered at him. "He *was* Pope John. Sigismund arrested him. Just yesterday he was tried at the council. The cardinals found him guilty of fifty-four crimes."

"What!" Hus scrambled to get up, scattering his papers.

"And he admitted he gave the order to arrest you, though he had pretended otherwise."

"Then I must be released!"

"No, you are to be tried by the council as planned."

"The council cannot proceed without the pope."

"The cardinals have decided that as a group, their authority is greater even than the pope's."

"Yet they accuse me of being anti-pope!" Hus frowned, his heavy brows drawn. "Why are you telling me all this?"

His informant opened his fist, revealing a burnished coin in his palm. "Your friend has excellent taste in bribes." He pulled a crumpled sheet of paper from his belt and tossed it down on the stones.

"What friend?" demanded Hus.

"Read it and find out!" snapped the guard. The door shut with a heavy clang.

Hus strained against the chain, feeling the stretch between his shoulder blades as his fingers closed over the note.

Beloved Master Hus, it began. *Peter, Wenceslas, and I work tirelessly for you to get your day in court. Sigismund has heard from the nobles of Prague—myself included—and they are demanding that you be given a public hearing. This charming guard has agreed to bring me your response if you give it to him. I beg to know how you fare. Your devoted but unsuccessful protector, Lord John of Chlum.*

He found his quill and hastily scratched a reply.

The council finally agreed to grant him a hearing in the dining hall of one of the monasteries. Benches had been arranged in a square facing a stack of books at the center. King Sigismund arrived with the cardinals in tow, representatives from all over Europe. They filed into the benches, their broad-rimmed red hats bobbing as they found their seats.

"So this is the John Hus who has caused so much trouble!" The king was looking him up and down. "You know Cardinal d'Ailly? He will be presiding over this council, now that Pope John is out of the picture."

He took a seat as the tall, clean-shaven cardinal came forward.

Cardinal d'Ailly pressed the palms of his long hands together and spoke loudly. "John Hus, are these the books you have written?"

"They are mine."

"You consider yourself a reformer?"

"There are many who are concerned about the purity of Christ's church. I am only one of them."

"You are charged with teaching the heresy of Doctor Wyclif. Do you affirm his teachings?"

"I do not hold to Wyclif's forty-five articles. I do not believe they can be condemned using Scripture, but I do not teach them."

Cardinal Zabarella stepped forward. "You are lying. I have read these teachings in your books."

Hus returned his steady gaze. "Then you cannot read."

"Your writings reject the authority of the pope!"

"They do not. I teach that Christ is the head of the church and that no pope who is corrupt has authority over the church."

"See! He denies the pope's authority. Recant!"

"I cannot recant that which I never believed. It would be a lie."

Cardinal d'Ailly leaned forward. "You are incapable of error?"

"Of course not! I am willing to recant of any errors, if you show me them from Scripture. But that is not what you are doing. You are demanding that I recant simply because the council says so! You have set yourselves up as an authority higher than Scripture."

The council pelted him with questions. He tried to answer each one clearly, but the next question was shouted before he could finish.

"Just say yes or no," ordered Cardinal Zabarella. "We don't care to hear your long explanations!"

Hus turned to the king in exasperation. "The council refuses to let me explain my beliefs, but when I deny their false accusations, they charge me with lying! How is this a fair hearing?"

"Do you accuse this council of error?" demanded Cardinal d'Ailly.

"Didn't you err when you elected Pope John? This very council found him guilty of dozens of crimes. Now he sits in prison!"

The council members came to their feet. Sigismund was already facing the prisoner, his face inches away. "Master Hus, you must submit yourself to this council. Will you not ask for their mercy?"

"I will not admit to false accusations."

"I cannot defend your heresy," warned the king. "I believe in the church's authority even if you don't. If you refuse to accept the judgment of this council, you will be condemned as a heretic. I will light the fire to burn you myself!"

The council members were all shouting at one another.

"I cannot examine this man in such chaos," declared Cardinal d'Ailly. "We will continue this later." He ordered the soldiers to take Hus back to his cell.

Two days later, the council called for him again. They asked the same questions. Hus gave the same answers. Furious, they sent him back to prison.

Lord John and Lord Wenceslas visited him a few days later in his cell.

"My protectors!" he cried. "How did you get in here?"

"Sigismund granted permission," explained Wenceslas.

Lord John ground his teeth. "After all he has done, he better not refuse such a simple request."

"It is good to see you, friends."

"I cannot believe they are holding you here with the rats!" said Lord John, pacing the small cell. "And what is the point of chains where there are a dozen guards outside the door?"

Hus just smiled at him.

"We were told you sent the council a letter refusing to recant," said Wenceslas.

The priest nodded. "They sent me a list of the charges against me and demanded that I admit to the charges and throw myself at their mercy. I will not allow them to lie about me."

"They will burn you at the stake if you refuse," said Lord John quietly.

"I have repeatedly said that if they would show me my errors from Scripture, I would accept their correction. But I would rather be burned than admit to heresies I have not committed!"

"You must follow the dictates of your heart," agreed Wenceslas. "But surely you could ask for mercy?"

Tears welled up in the prisoner's eyes. He shook his head. "Thank you, my friends. But my fate is sealed since they refuse to believe me. My execution is near. You will stay in Constance, won't you? It would be nice to have my friends with me at the end."

"We will stay," promised Lord John.

Hus stooped and collected a stack of papers at his feet. "Would you see that these letters are sent? There are many people to whom I would like to say good bye."

They left the tower with stacks of letters and heavy hearts.

It was a month before the council sent for him again. They carried him into the cathedral, where King Sigismund and the cardinals were waiting. Hus was forced to sit behind the table while the charges against him were read.

"I have already declared that I do not believe those things!" cried Hus, struggling to his feet. The guards forced him back down.

"Be silent!" Cardinal d'Ailly's voice rang through the hall. "John Hus, you are charged with being a supporter of the heretic John Wyclif. You refuse to listen to this council and admit your errors. Therefore, your writings are to be burned and you are to be stripped of your position as a priest."

"Give me instruction from Scripture!" he protested.

The guards held him in place while the council members shaved his head. One of the bishops carried a paper hat. Hus gasped when he saw the three devils painted on it above the word *heretic*.

"We commit your soul to the devil!" announced the bishop, shoving the hat down over the priest's ears.

"And I commit it to my merciful Lord Jesus Christ!" replied Hus, holding his head high.

Sigismund stood. "He has been condemned as a heretic. Deliver him to the executioners."

They paraded him out of the cathedral and through the city. A screaming crowd followed them past the cemetery, where his books were being tossed into a bonfire. Curled bits of ash rained down.

"Master Hus!" yelled Peter.

He searched the crowd. *There they are!* Peter, Wenceslas, and Lord John were running alongside as close as the guards would let them. *My friends have stayed with me to the end.*

He was knocked to the ground. A rusty chain was looped around his neck and wrapped to a stake.

"Stand firm, Master Hus!"

He found his friends again. "My Lord had a greater chain to bear than this!" he called to them.

Bundles of sticks and straw were piled around him.

The executioner loomed over him with a burning torch,

and offered him a last chance to save himself. "Heretic, do you recant?"

The people were so quiet, Hus could hear nothing but the crackling torch. He raised himself up on his elbows. "You can cook this goose, but there will come a swan after me who you will not be able to silence. Christ *will* restore the purity of his church!"

The executioner touched the torch to the pile of straw.

Lord John dropped his sword and fell to his knees, weeping. Above the sputtering flames, he heard the priest singing a familiar hymn. "Christ, thou son of the living God, have mercy on us." The voice soon faded.

The knight felt a hand on his shoulder. It was Peter.

"There is still something we can do, Lord John."

"What is that?"

"We can tell all of Prague—no, all of Bohemia and Hungary!— what has happened here. They destroyed the master's body, but they cannot destroy the truth."

Lord John allowed the boy to help him to his feet. With renewed hope, the three friends joined the retreating crowd, the flames dying out behind them.

Like the early church martyrs killed at the hands of the Roman emperors, Hus' death at the hands of the cardinals made the church take notice of his cause. The common people of Bohemia rose up against King Sigismund in a civil war, demanding church reform. The new pope declared the "Hussites" heretics and called a Crusade against Prague. Thousands died, including, eventually, King Sigismund himself.

A century later, John Hus' teachings would inspire a German monk named Martin Luther to become the most famous reformer in the history of the church. The Reformation *was about to begin.*

Other Medieval Christians

THE CHARACTERS IN this book are not the only significant Christians of the medieval era. Below is a brief look at several others.

The Venerable Bede was the first English historian, known for his book *Ecclesiastical History of the English Nation*. Little is known about the details of his life. He was born around 673 and was sent to a monastery by age seven. There he spent his entire life, devoting himself to the study of Scripture and observing his duties. He became a deacon at nineteen and died in 735.

Hildegard Von Bingen was born to a noble family in 1098 and was educated in a Benedictine convent from age eight. She quickly proved to have a brilliant mind and was made abbess of a convent in Disibodenberg, which she later moved to Bingen. Around 1150 she founded a new convent nearby. Hildegard was a popular mystic who claimed to receive visions from God. She was well respected in the church, and kings, bishops, and popes all came to her for advice. She is one of the first medieval women to write about medicine and serve as a doctor. She also wrote plays to be performed at her convent, composed music, and wrote poetry. She died in 1179.

Peter Lombard was an influential theologian who taught at the Cathedral School of Paris. Born in 1100, he is best known for his book, *Sentences*, a collection of quotations from the church fathers with his comments. This style of writing became popular after Lombard. The *Sentences* was a standard university text until Thomas Aquinas' *Summa Theologica* replaced it. Lombard became bishop of Paris one year before his death in 1160.

Peter Abelard was a controversial character in the medieval church. He was born in Britain in 1079 and studied at the Cathedral School of Paris. His most famous volume, titled *Yes and No*, led to a confrontation with Thomas Aquinas. Beyond his controversial beliefs, Abelard is best known for his scandalous relationship with Héloise, the well-educated niece of a high-ranking churchman. He died in 1160.

Bonaventure was born near Viterbo in 1221 and studied theology at the University of Paris, where he later taught theology for a short time. He eventually joined the Franciscan order. Among his writings are a commentary on Peter Lombard's *Sentences* and a book on the journey of the soul toward God. In 1273, a year before his death, he became cardinal archbishop of Albano.

John Duns Scotus was a Franciscan priest born in Scotland in 1266. He studied at Oxford and Paris and became a lecturer at both universities. As a philosopher and theologian, Scotus modified the teachings of the Greek philosopher Aristotle (384 B.C.-322 B.C.) and developed his own system of thought that was adopted by many of his students. He died in Cologne in 1308.

Christine de Pisan was born in Venice, Italy, in 1364 and raised in Paris. When her husband Etienne Castel, the king's secretary, died in 1389, she was left to raise three children by herself with no income. To make ends meet, she wrote and sold poetry and popular books on issues like the role of women in society and the church. In 1418 she retired to a convent and continued her writing until her death in 1429.

Joan of Arc is probably the most famous medieval woman. Born to a farmer in Domrémy, France, in 1412, during the conflict known as the Hundred Years War, Joan believed she was called by God to free France from English control. In her white armor, this warrior-mystic was given control of an army and led a charge that made history. She forced the English army to retreat at Orléans but was captured at Compiègne and put on trial in 1431. The English court found her guilty of sorcery and heresy and ordered her to be burned at the stake. Twenty-five years after her death, another court overturned the conviction, declaring Joan a hero and a saint. Her fame is a good example of the ever-changing roles of women in church history.

Johannes Gutenberg was born to a merchant in Mainz, Germany, around 1400, and died in 1467. He is known as the inventor of moveable type printing in Europe. The Chinese had been using a similar form of printing since around 1040, but knowledge of this method had not yet reached much of Europe. Gutenberg's first press in Strasbourg was financed by Johann Fust, but their partnership ended when Fust sued Gutenberg and won, taking all the printing equipment. Gutenberg later set up a second press with another investor. He produced the now rare Gutenberg Bible, of which only forty-two copies have survived. The Gutenberg press published books much faster than they could be copied by hand. This development allowed Protestant ideas to spread quicker during the Reformation and launched centuries of technological advances.

The Renaissance: The Middle Ages Come to an End

ART, CULTURE, AND religion were alive during the Middle Ages. But life was hard. The common people worked from sunrise to sunset just to feed their families. They had little time to read or sculpt or paint. Only the wealthy could indulge in those pursuits. But as the nobles lost some of their power to the rising middle class, more people began to explore art and science. Their interests led to a new period in history called the *Renaissance*.

The Renaissance began in northern Italy in the fifteenth century. The city of Florence, under the leadership of the powerful de Medici family, promoted advances in the arts and sciences. During the previous century, Florence had suffered under the reign of Pope Gregory XI. But the de Medici family began putting money back into the city, supporting artists and musicians and inventors. They gave the city a new life that spread to all of Europe.

During the Renaissance, people began to read classic Greek books again. Ancient sculptures and paintings were discovered in the ruins of old cities. Painters and poets began exploring humanity and nature in their art. Leonardo da Vinci (1452-1519) painted the *Mona Lisa*, shaped beautiful sculptures, designed buildings, and even made detailed plans for a flying machine. Johannes Gutenberg invented the printing press, printing the famous Gutenberg Bible in 1453. Explorers like Christopher Columbus (1451-1506) and Bartholomew Diaz (who died in 1500) discovered parts of the globe Europe had never known.

Education was no longer limited to the cathedral schools or monasteries. Universities were founded all over Europe, teaching medicine and law. A movement called the *New Learning* encouraged women to learn Latin and Greek, and more women began to write books.

Many traditional doctrines of the church were questioned. People everywhere called for the church to reform its practices and teachings, although they did not agree on how it should be done. The Renaissance would soon open the door for a German monk named Martin Luther (1483-1546) to lead the world into the era of the *Protestant Reformation*.

Author Information

Mindy and Brandon Withrow are writers and active bloggers who have lived most recently in Philadelphia, Pennsylvania and Birmingham, Alabama. Brandon is adjunct professor of church history at Beeson Divinity School. They are both graduates of the Moody Bible Institute in Chicago; Brandon is also a graduate of Trinity Evangelical Divinity School and has a PhD in Historical Theology from Westminster Theological Seminary. One of their favorite activities is reading to their nieces and nephews.

LOOK OUT FOR OTHER BOOKS IN THE SERIES

Peril and Peace:
Chronicles of the Ancient Church
History Lives, Volume 1
ISBN: 978-1-84550-082-5

Read the stories of Paul, Polycarp, Justin, Origen, Cyprian, Constantine, Athanasius, Ambrose, Augustine, John Chrysostom, Jerome, Patrick, and Benedict, and discover the roots of Christianity. In their lives you will see the young and developing church struggling and growing in a hostile and difficult world.

Courage and Conviction:
Chronicles of the Reformation Church
History Lives, Volume 3
ISBN: 978-1-84550-222-5

Read the stories of the reformers in the 16th and 17th centuries who changed the face of the Christian church forever. Meet the German monk, the French scholar, and the Scottish tutor who protested corruption in the church. Get to know the queens and explorers who risked everything for the freedom to worship according to their consciences.

Hearts and Hands:
Chronicles of the Awakening Church
History Lives, Volume 4
ISBN: 978-1-84550-288-1

Read the stories of the gifted preachers and justice fighters who led the 1st & 2nd Great Awakenings in the 18th and 19th centuries. From John Wesley and Jonathan Edwards to Elizabeth Fry and Harriet Beecher Stowe, God used the tender hearts and strong hands of his people to offer mercy to the world.

WHERE WE GOT OUR INFORMATION
AND OTHER HELPFUL RESOURCES

Case, Shirley Jackson. *Makers of Christianity: From Jesus to Charlemagne.* New York: Holt and Company, 1934.

Cavallini, Guiliana. *Catherine of Sienna: The Dialogue.* New York: Paulist Press, 1980.

Cross, Samuel Hazzard and Olgerd P. Sherbowitz-Wetzor. *The Russian Primary Chronicle: Laurentian Text.* Cambridge, MA.: Medieval Academy of America, 1953.

Cunningham, Mary. *Faith in the Byzantine World.* Downers Grove, IL: InterVarsity Press, 2002.

Dictionary of the Middle Ages. 13 Vols. Joseph Strayer, ed. New York: Charles Scribner's, 1982-1989.

Dvornik, Francis. *Byzantine Missions Among the Slavs: SS. Constantine-Cyril and Methodius.* New Brunswick, NJ: Rutgers University Press, 1970.

Emerton, Ephraim, trans. *The Letters of Saint Boniface.* New York: Columbia University Press, 1940.

Evans, G. R. *Bernard of Clairvaux.* Great Medieval Thinkers series. Brian Davies, general editor. Oxford: Oxford University Press, 2000.

Fines, John. *Who's Who in the Middle Ages.* New York: Barnes & Noble Books, 1995.

Galli, Mark. *Francis of Assisi and His World.* Downers Grove, IL: InterVarsity Press, 2002.

Godfrey, John. *The Church in Anglo-Saxon England.* Cambridge: Cambridge University Press, 1962.

Grant, A. J., editor. *Early Lives of Charlemagne.* London: Chatto & Windus, 1926.

Hall, Louis Brewer. *The Perilous Vision of John Wyclif.* Chicago: Nelson-Hall, 1983.

House, Adrian. *Francis of Assisi*. Mahwah, NJ: HiddenSpring, 2000.

James, Bruno S. *Saint Bernard of Clairvaux*. New York: Harper and Brothers, 1957.

Konstam, Angus. *Historical Atlas of the Crusades*. New York: Checkmark Books, 2002.

Langley, Andrew. *Medieval Life*. Eyewitness Books series. New York: DK Publishing, 2004.

Luddy, Ailbe J. *Life and Teaching of St. Bernard*. Dublin: M. H. Gill and Son, 1937.

Markus, R.A. *Gregory the Great and His World*. Cambridge: Cambridge University Press, 1997.

New Catholic Encyclopedia. 15 Vols. Detroit, MI: Thomson Gale, 2003.

Peterson, Susan Lynn. *Timeline Charts of the Western Church*. Grand Rapids: Zondervan, 1999.

Richards, Jeffrey. *Consul of God: The Life and Times of Gregory the Great*. London: Routledge & Kegan Paul, 1980.

Rigg, J. M. *St. Anselm of Canterbury: A Chapter in the History of Religion*. London: Methuen & Co., 1896.

Schaff, Philip. *The History of the Christian Church*, Vols. 4-6. Grand Rapids, MI: Eerdmans, 1910.

Southern, R.W. *Saint Anselm and His Biographer: A Study of His Monastic Life and Thought*. Cambridge: Cambridge University Press, 1963.

Spinka, Matthew. *John Hus: A Biography*. Princeton, NJ: Princeton University Press, 1968.

Spinka, Matthew. *John Hus at the Council of Constance*. New York: Columbia University Press, 1965.

Tachiaos, Anthony-Emil N. *Cyril and Methodius of Thessalonica: The Acculturation of the Slavs*. Crestwood, NY: St. Vladimir's Seminary Press, 2001.

Verdnadsky, George. *Kievan Russia*. New Haven, CT: Yale University Press, 1948.

Webb, Geoffrey and Adrian Walker, trans. *St. Bernard of Clairvaux*. London: A. R. Mowbray & Co, 1960.

Weisheipl, James A. *Friar Thomas D'Aquino: His Life, Thought, and Work*. Garden City, NY: Doubleday, 1974.

Willibald. *The Life of Saint Boniface*. Translated by George W. Robinson. Cambridge, MA: Harvard University Press, 1916.

NORTH SEA

Oxford London
Thames Canterbury
ENGLISH CHANNEL

HESSE REGION
Paderborn
Cologne
HOLY ROMAN EMPIRE
Rhine
Paris
Frankfurt
Prague
Clairvaux
Vézelay
Constance Alps
Rhone
Lyons
Avignon
Florence
ADRIATIC S
Sienna
Assisi
Rome Monte Cassino
Naples

ME

The World of the Medieval Church

CHRISTIAN FOCUS PUBLICATIONS

Christian Focus | Christian Heritage | CF4K | Mentor

Christian Focus Publications publishes books for adults and children under its four main imprints: Christian Focus, CF4K, Mentor and Christian Heritage. Our books reflect that God's word is reliable and Jesus is the way to know him, and live for ever with him.

Our children's publication list includes a Sunday school curriculum that covers pre-school to early teens; puzzle and activity books. We also publish personal and family devotional titles, biographies and inspirational stories that children will love.

If you are looking for quality Bible teaching for children then we have an excellent range of Bible story and age specific theological books.

From pre-school to teenage fiction, we have it covered!

Find us at our web page:
www.christianfocus.com

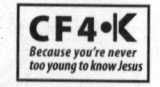

CF4•K
Because you're never too young to know Jesus